FIRST STEPS IN
Academic Writing

Ann Hogue

Longman

First Steps in Academic Writing

Copyright © 1996 by Addison-Wesley Publishing Company, Inc.

Addison-Wesley Longman, 10 Bank Street, White Plains, N.Y. 10606

Editorial Director:	Joanne Dresner
Acquisitions Editor:	Allen Ascher
Development Editor:	Françoise Leffler
Production Editorial:	Lisa Hutchins
Text Design:	PC&F, Inc.
Cover Design:	Curt Belshe
Text Art:	PC&F, Inc.

Grateful acknowledgment is given to the following for granting permission to reproduce photos:
Page 1, Jeroboam Inc.; Page 15, BETTMANN; Page 33, Caroline Gibbs; Page 68, © Chlaus Lotscher, from ALASKA STOCK; Page 134, Arthur Griffen; Page 173, both photos from AP/WIDE WORLD PHOTOS.

Library of Congress Cataloging-in-Publication Data

Hogue, Ann.
    First steps in academic writing / Ann Hogue.
        p.   cm.
    Includes index.
    ISBN 0-201-83410-3
      1. English language—Rhetoric. 2. Academic writing. I. Title.
PE1478.H57   1995
808'. 042—dc20   95-24399
                                      CIP

15 16 17 18 19 20 – CRS – 0706050403

Contents

Introduction

First Steps in Academic Writing is intended for high-beginning writing students of English as a second language. It takes beginning writers from understanding the concept of a paragraph (Unit 1) to writing three basic types of paragraphs: chronological process (Unit 2), spatial description (Unit 3), and listing (Unit 4). Unit 5 shows students how to use examples, and Unit 6 shows how to express and support their opinions. In these last two units, the forms for personal letters and business letters are also taught.

Examples of real writing abound. Exercises and writing assignments are contextualized to make them more engaging to the student and to reinforce the notion of writing as discourse. An effort has been made to limit the vocabulary load, but in a few cases glosses help students understand the potentially unfamiliar words that were retained in the interest of providing engaging models and exercises. Verb tenses are also limited to those that beginning students are likely to be comfortable with.

Aims of the Text

Woven into every chapter are the four aims of the text:
- To offer a structured approach to writing
- To acquaint students with the process of writing
- To provide practice in basic sentence structure
- To develop grammar and mechanical skills

Structured Approach

First Steps in Academic Writing offers a carefully controlled, structured approach to writing by teaching the standard three-part English paragraph using the three basic organizational modes mentioned earlier: chronological order, spatial order, and a type of organization called "listing" order. Students learn to develop paragraphs using specific descriptive details, reasons, and examples. For each rhetorical form—be it topic sentences, transition signals, or specific descriptive details—numerous models, examples, and exercises are provided for the students to analyze and manipulate before they are expected to create it on their own.

Each unit has at least two, and usually three, writing assignments so that the students practice the same mode several times. The first writing assignment in each unit is usually based on the chapter's opening activity, in which students work in pairs or teams to develop material for the later writing assignment. The second and third assignments deal with the same mode using different topics. All assignments are single paragraphs (or letters). In addition, each unit ends with several suggestions for additional writing practice, which may be assigned as ungraded writing or journal writing.

The Process of Writing

Each unit carefully takes students through the various steps in writing: Prewriting for ideas, outlining, drafting, revising, and editing lead to carefully written final drafts. Peer-editing techniques are among the several types of activities that offer opportunities for pair and group work. Recommended procedures for writing activities are outlined below.

Basic Sentence Structure

The sentence-structure sections of each unit progressively introduce simple, compound, and complex sentences. The writing practice in each sentence-structure section is a sentence-combining exercise in which the students can manipulate the structure they have been learning in a controlled, contextualized environment.

Grammar and Mechanical Skills

Complementary to the sentence-structure section in each unit is a grammar and mechanics section, which deals with such skills as finding subjects and verbs and using punctuation and capitalization correctly.

Recommended Procedure for Writing Assignments

The recommended procedure for writing assignments is as follows. The students should work in pairs or groups in the prewriting stage, by themselves in the writing stages, and in pairs again in the editing stage. In my experience, students have difficulty developing ideas to write about in isolation. Therefore, I recommend that the brainstorming and outlining steps be done in pairs, triads, or at the beginning of the term when the students need the most teacher guidance, with the whole class participating.

Armed with the results of prewriting—more or less a detailed outline—the students can write their paragraphs on their own either in class or at home.

The next step is editing, and it is important to convey to the students the need to do all parts of the editing step. First, students check their own work both for meaning and for mechanics (grammar, punctuation, and sentence structure). Then they bring their writing to class and ask a classmate to check it—again for both meaning and mechanics. Each writing assignment is accompanied by a "Paragraph Checklist," which students should use to check their own and each other's work. You may find it helpful to duplicate copies of the checklists in advance and ask students to clip one to each assignment. This may encourage them to be conscientious about the editing step.

Writing the final draft is to be done individually. After you process the final drafts, encourage students to rewrite the paragraph. Some instructors allow rewrites on most paragraphs but only a certain number of them. The students must receive a passing mark on the no-rewrite assignments in order to pass the course. It is an individual decision whether you give a grade on the first copy handed in and then raise that grade on each rewrite, or whether you make comments and/or corrections on the first copy and then grade the rewrite. I personally am still searching for a satisfactory method of dealing with rewrites and grades.

Finally, I recommend that students do much of their writing in class. Beginning writers in particular benefit from having the support of a teacher and classmates during the often excruciating process of putting pen to paper.

Appendixes

Five appendixes are included at the back of the book. The first three—Correction Symbols, Conjunctions, and Transition Signals—are intended primarily as reference lists for students. The last two—Word Division and Parts of Speech—can be used as instructional lessons as well.

Acknowledgments

Thanks to many people are in order. Producing a new textbook is a laborious pursuit. Without the assistance of colleagues and the encouragement of editors, it would be even more so. Thanks, therefore, to colleagues Linda Moyer and Barbara Bonander, who tried out various sections of the book in their classes. I am particularly indebted to Caroline Gibbs of the Intensive English Program at the College of Marin, who tested the entire book and provided excellent suggestions for improvements. Thanks also to my editors, Allen Ascher, Françoise Leffler, and Lisa Hutchins, of Addison-Wesley/Longman.

Finally, thanks to my students, who continue to challenge and inspire me and who teach me something new every day. Special thanks to Anh Nguyen for allowing me to use his excellent paragraph as a model in Unit 1.

Unit **1**

Introducing People

ORGANIZATION

- *Paragraph Form*

GRAMMAR AND MECHANICS

- *What Is a Sentence?*

- *Subjects and Verbs*

- *End-of-Sentence Punctuation*

- *Capitalization: Five Rules*

SENTENCE STRUCTURE

- *Simple Sentences*

- *Connecting Words:* and, or

- *Sentence Combining*

THE WRITING PROCESS

- *Freewriting*

- *Editing*

Prewriting: Taking Notes

Whenever you write, you first need to have some ideas to write about. Taking notes is one way to gather ideas. In this activity, you will ask a classmate some questions and take notes about his or her answers. When you take notes, you do not have to write complete sentences. Just write down the important information.

ACTIVITY

1. Look at the chart below. With your class, make up questions about the topics to ask a classmate. Discuss which questions are OK to ask and which personal questions you should not ask. Your teacher will write the questions on the chalkboard.

Sample questions:	Sample notes:
What is your first name?	Santy
What is your family name?	Valverde
Where are you from?	Michoacan, Mexico
How long have you lived in the United States?	two years

2. Choose a partner and ask him or her the questions. Take notes by writing the answers in the chart. Keep the chart. You will use it later to write a paragraph about your classmate.

3. Introduce your classmate by telling his or her answers to the class or to a small group.

OK	Not OK	Information	Notes (Classmate's Answers)
✔	☐	First name and family name	_____
☐	✘	Age	_____
☐	☐	City and country	_____
☐	☐	Family status	_____
☐	☐	Religion	_____
☐	☐	Address in the United States	_____
☐	☐	Length of time in the United States	_____
☐	☐	Length of time studying English	_____
☐	☐	Reasons for studying English	_____
☐	☐	Job or occupation	_____
☐	☐	Salary	_____
☐	☐	Hobbies or sports	_____
☐	☐	Weekend activities	_____
☐	☐	Plans for the future	_____

(You and your class may add other questions.)

PART **1** Organization

Paragraph Form

A **paragraph** is a group of related sentences about a single topic. The topic of a paragraph is one, and only one, idea. The first word in a paragraph is moved to the right about one-half inch. This is called **indenting** the first word. Also, there is blank space down both the left and the right sides of the page. These blank spaces are called **margins.**

Each paragraph that you write for this class should have a **title.** A title tells the topic of the paragraph in a few words. A title is short. It may even be one word. A title is usually not a complete sentence.

Examples:
My Classmate
Friendship
My Best Friend
How to Play American Football
Shopping for a Used Car

Here are some rules for writing paragraphs for this class:

1. Write the title of your paragraph on the top line.

2. Leave margins (blank spaces) of about an inch down the left and right sides of your paper. Don't write to the edge of the page.

3. Skip a line, and begin writing on the third line.

4. Indent the first sentence about one-half inch from the left margin.

5. Begin each sentence at the end of the preceding one. (Don't start each new sentence on a new line.)

6. Write on every other line. Writing on every other line leaves space for your teacher to make corrections and write comments.

7. If a word is too long to fit at the end of a line, write the whole word on the next writing line. Don't try to divide a long word unless you know the rules for doing so. Guidelines for dividing words are given in Appendix D at the back of the book.

MODEL PARAGRAPH

When you write a paragraph, make it look like this:

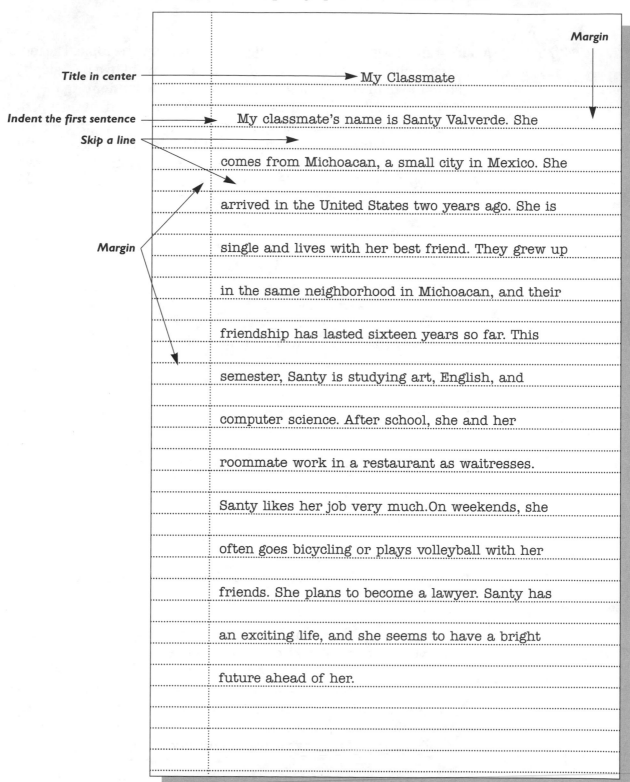

Margin

Title in center ────────────► My Classmate

Indent the first sentence ────────►   My classmate's name is Santy Valverde. She

Skip a line ────────►

comes from Michoacan, a small city in Mexico. She

arrived in the United States two years ago. She is

Margin   single and lives with her best friend. They grew up

in the same neighborhood in Michoacan, and their

friendship has lasted sixteen years so far. This

semester, Santy is studying art, English, and

computer science. After school, she and her

roommate work in a restaurant as waitresses.

Santy likes her job very much. On weekends, she

often goes bicycling or plays volleyball with her

friends. She plans to become a lawyer. Santy has

an exciting life, and she seems to have a bright

future ahead of her.

PRACTICE:
Paragraph Form

Work by yourself or with a partner.

1. Find the mistakes in the form of this paragraph.

2. Copy it using correct form on an 8½-by-11-inch piece of notebook paper. It should be *one* paragraph.

> My Classmate
>
> My classmate is Phuong Pham. She is from Vietnam.
> She came to California with her family in 1989.
> She is married.
> She lives with her husband, her children, and her parents-in-law in a house. Phuong is taking an art class, two English classes, computer science, and math.
> She likes to listen to music and to read books.
> She doesn't have a job but plans to when she finishes school.

WRITING PRACTICE 1 *Introducing a Classmate*

Write a paragraph about the classmate you interviewed in the activity on page 2. First, read about how to write a good paragraph.

The Writing Process: An Introduction

Good writing is more than just using correct grammar. It is also means thinking, planning, checking, and revising. In this book, you will become skilled writers by always using these four steps: (1) prewriting (getting ideas and organizing them), (2) writing the first draft, (3) editing the first draft (checking and correcting it), and (4) writing the final draft to hand in. In addition, your teacher may ask you to rewrite your final draft again after he or she has checked it.

STEP 1: Prewriting — Taking Notes

In the prewriting step, you gather ideas to write about. Taking notes is one way to gather ideas. Students take notes all the time. For example, students take notes from class lectures and from reading assignments. They may use their notes later to study for tests and to write papers. On page 2, you made notes when your classmate answered your questions. These are the notes you will use to write your paragraph.

STEP 2: Writing the First Draft

- Give your paragraph this title: *My Classmate.*
- Begin your paragraph with this sentence: *My classmate's name is* _____. (You may begin your paragraph with a different sentence if you want to.)
- Write several sentences telling about your classmate. Use your notes from the chart on page 2 to make sentences.
- End your paragraph with a sentence or two that tells how you feel about your classmate. For example, *I am happy to have* _____ *as my classmate. I think we will become good friends.*

STEP 3: Editing the First Draft

When you edit something, you check it and make changes and corrections. If you learn to edit well, you will write clearer, more interesting paragraphs that communicate your meaning.

There are several steps in the editing process.

- *First, check the meaning.* Read your paragraph silently to yourself. Does it communicate what you want it to? Is the meaning of all the sentences clear? If not, make changes.
- *Next, check the mechanics.* Read it silently again. This time look for mistakes in punctuation, grammar, and spelling. If you find any mistakes, fix them.
- *Third, have your partner check the meaning.* Read your paragraph aloud to your partner. Ask your partner if any information is incorrect or if any sentences are unclear. If the answer is yes, make changes.
- *Finally, have your partner check the mechanics.* Ask your partner to read your paragraph silently and to check it for mistakes in punctuation and spelling. If he or she finds any mistakes, fix them. If you and your partner don't agree about a possible mistake, ask a third student or the teacher.

PARTNERS: When your classmate reads his or her paragraph out loud, listen well. If something is not clear to you, ask your classmate to explain it more clearly to you. Then suggest a way to make it clearer in writing. When you read the paragraph silently and check it for spelling and punctuation, don't correct anything you are not sure about. Finally, it is also a good idea to find one or two positive things to say about your classmate's paragraph. You can comment on the interesting content, the neat writing, the good grammar, or anything else that is good.

STEP 4:
Writing the Final Draft

Write a neat final draft of your paragraph to hand in to the teacher. Be sure that you use correct paragraph form.

PART 2 Grammar and Mechanics

What Is a Sentence?

How do you know what a sentence is? You will learn more about sentences later, but for now, you should know this definition:

> A **sentence** is a group of words that contains a subject and a verb and expresses a complete thought.

These are sentences:

1. He is a student.
2. Speed kills.
3. It's hot today.
4. He looks tired.
5. Are you hungry?
6. Who's there?
7. The man bought a new car.
8. Does your sister live with you?
9. Where did you buy your new car?
10. Hurry! *(The subject in this sentence is "you.")*

These are not sentences:

11. Hot weather. *(There is no verb.)*
12. The man bought. *(This is not a complete thought.)*
13. Because it rained. *(This is not a complete thought.)*
14. Is very handsome. *(There is no subject.)*
15. Every morning before breakfast. *(There is no subject or verb.)*

PRACTICE:
Recognizing Sentences

Work with a partner.

1. Read each group of words out loud.

2. Decide which ones are complete sentences and which ones are not.

3. Write *yes* next to the complete sentences and *no* next to the nonsentences.

4. Explain why the nonsentences are not sentences.

   Examples:

   __no__ Is very hot today. (_____ There is no subject. _____)

   __yes__ It is very hot today. (_____)

1. _____ My new classmate from Brazil. (_____)

2. _____ He speaks three languages fluently. (_____)

3. _____ Is very handsome. (_____)

4. _____ When he arrived here. (_____)

5. _____ He wants to start his own business. (_____)

6. _____ He isn't married. (_____)

7. _____ Enjoys many sports, especially soccer. (_____)

8. _____ Don't worry! (_____)

9. _____ Help! (_____)

10. _____ They didn't like. (_____)

11. _____ Because they are new students. (_____)

12. _____ They don't want. (_____)

Subjects and Verbs

Every sentence must have at least one subject and one verb in order to be a sentence. Some sentences must have other parts in order to express a complete thought. *The man bought* is not a sentence because it does not express a complete thought. We need to know what he bought.

Subjects and verbs are the most important parts of a sentence. In English, the subject of a sentence is *always* expressed except in a command: *Hurry!* (We know that the subject is "you.")

> The **subject** tells who or what did something. It is a noun or pronoun.

My roommate lost the keys to his car.
(Who lost the keys?—my roommate)

The car hit the pedestrian.
(What hit the pedestrian?—the car)

Skiing and snowboarding are my favorite winter sports.
(What are my favorite winter sports?—skiing and snowboarding)

> The **verb** often tells the action. However, sometimes a verb doesn't tell an action. Sometimes it just links the subject with the rest of the sentence.

Action verbs
The car <u>hit</u> the pedestrian.
My family <u>lives</u> in a two-bedroom apartment.
My roommate <u>lost</u> his car keys.
His girlfriend <u>found</u> them.

Linking verbs
Snow skiing <u>is</u> my favorite winter sport.
I <u>feel</u> sick.
You <u>look</u> hungry.
I <u>am</u> lucky that my roommate <u>is</u> a good cook.

The most common linking verbs are *be, become, feel, look, seem, smell, sound,* and *taste.*

PRACTICE:
Finding Subjects and Verbs

Work with a partner.

1. Underline the subjects with one line.

2. Underline the verbs with two lines.

3. Write S or V above each underlined word.

Examples:

      S   V
<u>My little brother</u> <u>is</u> in the fifth grade.

 S   V   V
<u>He</u> <u>watches</u> TV and <u>does</u> his homework at the same time.

1. My best friend is single.

2. He likes his job but hates his boss.

3. He didn't go to work yesterday.

4. This semester, he is studying English and computer science.

5. He and I don't have any classes together.

6. He speaks and understands English very well.

7. On weekends, he and his friends play soccer.

8. He doesn't have a steady girlfriend yet.

9. Smile!

10. Be happy!

11. Don't worry!

End-of-Sentence Punctuation

> A sentence ends with a period (.), an exclamation point (!), or a question mark (?).

A sentence normally ends with a period. If a sentence is a question, use a question mark.

> Where do you live?
> Are you married or single?
> We don't have any homework tonight, do we?

You can use an exclamation point after words, phrases, or sentences to show strong emotion and after an urgent command.

> Wow!
> What a nice surprise!
> We were really scared!
> Help!

PRACTICE:
End-of-Sentence Punctuation

Work by yourself or with a partner. Place a period, a question mark, or an exclamation point at the end of each sentence.

Examples:
How many languages do you speak?
I speak only one.

1. How long has she been in the United States

2. She has been in the United States for only six months

3. In English, the subject is always expressed except in commands

(continued on the next page)

4. Stop that robber

5. Did anyone see the accident

6. The airport was so crowded that we almost missed our plane

7. Are you going to hand in your homework

8. You're going to hand in your homework, aren't you

9. It's an earthquake

10. Get under your desks

PRACTICE:
Punctuating Sentences

Work by yourself or with a partner.

1. Decide where sentences begin and end in this paragraph. (There are fourteen sentences.)

2. Add punctuation at the end of each sentence.

3. Change the first letter of each new sentence to a capital.

© The Walt Disney Company

> ### Introducing Myself
>
> My name is Mickey Mouse. I live in a place called Disney-land my father's name is Walt Disney he was a famous cartoon-ist a cartoonist is a person who draws cartoon characters like me i was born about seventy years ago in a movie studio in Hollywood, California i first appeared in a cartoon in 1928 the name of the cartoon was "Steamboat Willie" at first I appeared in cartoons with Minnie Mouse soon my friends Donald Duck and Goofy joined me in addition to starring in cartoons, I also work at Disneyland there I stand around and smile a lot I also pose for pictures with visitors i enjoy my job a lot because I make children all over the world happy

Capitalization: Five Rules

In English, there are many rules for using capital letters. Here are five important ones.

RULES	**EXAMPLES**
Capitalize:	
1. The first word in a sentence	**M**y name is Mickey Mouse.
2. The pronoun *I* alone.	At first **I** appeared in cartoons
3. Names of people and their titles	**K**ing **F**aisal **P**resident **Y**eltsin **P**rofessor **I**ndiana **J**ones **M**r. and **M**rs. **H**omer **S**impson
BUT NOT a title without a name	He's a king. Have you met your math professor?
EXCEPTION: A title without a name is sometimes capitalized if it refers to a specific person.	The **P**resident of the **U**nited **S**tates had dinner with the **E**mperor of **J**apan.
4. Nationalities, languages, religions, and ethnic groups	**V**ietnamese **J**ewish **E**nglish **C**hristian **S**panish **A**sian **F**arsi **H**ispanic **N**ative **A**merican
NOTE: Don't capitalize school subjects except names of nationalities, languages, religions, and so forth.	calculus **R**ussian history computer science **R**ussian math **F**rench history **L**atin
5. Specific places you could find on a map	**L**ake **T**iticaca **E**ngland the **N**orth **P**ole **S**outh **A**merica **F**irst **S**treet **T**iananmen **S**quare

PRACTICE:
Capitalization

Work with a partner.

1. Write your own examples for capitalization rules 3–5.

2. Ask your teacher for help with spelling, or use a dictionary.

Rule 3

a queen _____

a president _____

a doctor _____

a mayor or
governor _____

Rule 4

a language _____

a nationality _____

an ethnic group _____

a religion _____

Rule 5

a street _____

a city or town _____

a state _____

a country _____

a sea or an ocean _____

an island _____

a lake _____

a river _____

a park _____

a square _____

PRACTICE:
Capitalization

Work by yourself or with a partner. Change the small letters to capital letters wherever necessary in the following paragraph.

$\overset{N}{\cancel{n}}$elson $\overset{M}{\cancel{m}}$andela

my name is nelson mandela, and i have had an unusual life. i have been both a prisoner and a president in my country. i was born in 1918 in the small village of qunu in the transkei, which is a large territory (like a state) in south africa. my father, henry mandela, was chief of our tribe, the tembus. as a child, i took care of the family's cattle and goats and fished in the bashee river near our village. i decided to become a lawyer because this seemed to be the best way to help my people. after i became a lawyer, i became the leader of a group of young africans who wanted to change the system of discrimination in our country. because of my political activities, i was arrested and sent to prison. i spent twenty-seven years in prison. i spent most of those years on roggen island, a cold, windy island in the atlantic ocean. the world didn't forget about me while i was in prison, however. i received important visitors, awards, and university degrees from all over the world. i also learned afrikaans, which is the language of white south africans. of course i also speak english and xhosa, which is the tembu language. at last, i was set free in 1990, and i became the president of south africa in 1994. now i will try to bring peace, democracy, and prosperity to all of my country's people.

WRITING PRACTICE 2 *Introducing Yourself*

Write a paragraph about yourself. Practice what you have learned about paragraph form, putting periods at the end of sentences, and capitalization.

Use the same four steps in writing this paragraph that you used in writing the paragraph about your classmate: take notes, write the first draft, edit it, and write the final draft to hand in.

STEP 1:
Prewriting—
Taking Notes

Write a brief answer to each question on the line provided. These are the notes you will use to write full sentences in the next step.

What is your complete name? _____

Where do you live? _____

When and where were you born? _____

What is your nationality? _____

What languages do you speak? _____

Where did you go to school before this school? _____

What were your favorite school subjects? _____

Did you study a foreign language in school? _____

Do you have any hobbies? _____

What do you do in your free time? _____

What are your plans for the future? _____

STEP 2:
Write the First
Draft

Now write your answers in complete sentences. Use correct paragraph form as in the model on page 4. Give your paragraph this title: *Introducing Myself.* Pay special attention to putting periods at the end of all your sentences and using capital letters correctly.

STEP 3:
Edit the First Draft

Follow these editing steps.
- *First, check the meaning.* Read your paragraph silently to yourself. Does it say what you want it to say about you? Is the meaning of all of the sentences clear? If not, make changes.

- *Next, check the mechanics.* Read it silently again. This time look for mistakes in punctuation, grammar, spelling, and capitalization. If you find any mistakes, fix them. Use the Paragraph Checklist below as a guide. Put a check next to every item on the list.
- *Third, have your partner check the meaning.* Read your paragraph aloud to your partner. Ask your partner if any sentences were not clear. If the answer is yes, make changes.
- *Finally, have your partner check the mechanics.* Ask your partner to read your paragraph silently and to check each item on the Paragraph Checklist. If he or she finds any mistakes, fix them. If you and your partner don't agree about a possible mistake, ask a third student or the teacher.

PARTNERS: As you did in Writing Practice 1, you will help your classmate write a clear, correct paragraph by your careful editing. First, listen to the paragraph. Does it make sense? Is it clear? Second, read it silently and check it against the Paragraph Checklist. Again, don't correct anything you are not sure about. And remember to make one or two positive comments about your classmate's writing skills!

PARAGRAPH CHECKLIST

FORM

✔ ✔ Check the paragraph form. (Does the paragraph look like the model on page 4?)

GRAMMAR AND MECHANICS

☐ ☐ Check for capital letters.

☐ ☐ Check the spelling.

☐ ☐ Is there a period at the end of all sentences?

SENTENCE STRUCTURE

☐ ☐ Check the sentences. Do they have at least one subject and one verb, and do they express a complete thought?

STEP 4:
Write the Final Draft

Write a neat final draft of your paragraph to hand in to the teacher.

PART 3 Sentence Structure

Earlier, you learned that a sentence is a group of words that contains at least one subject and one verb and expresses a complete thought. Now you will begin to learn about the different kinds of sentences in English.

There are four basic kinds of sentences in English: simple sentences, compound sentences, complex sentences, and compound-complex sentences.

Simple Sentences

> A **simple sentence** is a sentence that has one subject-verb combination.

The subject in a simple sentence may be compound (*My brother and I are completely different*). The verb may also be compound (*They laughed and cried at the same time*). What is important is that there is only one subject-verb combination in a simple sentence.

These are simple sentences. Notice that no commas are used in them.

1. My younger sister speaks English well.
2. My mother and father speak English well.
3. My older brother is a lawyer and has a good job.
4. My mother and father speak and write English well.

The simple sentences above can be written as formulas.
S V—simple subject with simple verb
SS V—compound subject with simple verb
S V V—simple subject with compound verb
SS V V—compound subject with compound verb

The following sentences are not simple sentences because they have two subject-verb combinations. They are **compound sentences,** and their formulas look like this: SV, (connecting word) SV. You will learn more about compound sentences in Unit 2.

My brother lives in New York, and my sister lives in Paris.

My older brother is a college graduate, but he can't find a job.

PRACTICE:
Simple Sentence Patterns

A. Work by yourself or with a partner. Identify the pattern in the following simple sentences.

1. Underline the subjects with one line.

2. Underline the verbs with two lines.

3. Write S or V above each underlined word.

4. Finally, write the formula for the sentence in the numbered space below.

Example:

$$S \qquad V \qquad\qquad V$$

My grandfather loves to fish and often takes me with him to his favorite fishing place.

Formula: ___S V V___

My Grandfather

[1]My grandfather is old in years but young in spirit. [2]Every day, he swims a mile and works in his garden. [3]He and my grandmother were married fifty years ago. [4]They have four children and ten grandchildren. [5]My grandfather loves parties and invites our entire family to his house for a big dinner on his birthday. [6]All twenty of us eat and tell stories half the night. [7]He never gets tired and is always the last to go to bed. [8]On his last birthday, my brothers and I gave him a present. [9]We all put our money together and bought him a video game system. [10]Now he wants us to come over to his house every weekend.

---

1. _____   3. _____   5. _____   7. _____   9. _____

2. _____   4. _____   6. _____   8. _____   10. _____

(continued on the next page)

B. Work first by yourself, and then with a partner.

   1. Write six simple sentences about your family or family members. Use each of these patterns twice: SV, SSV, SVV.

   2. Show your sentences to your partner. Ask your partner to identify the pattern in each sentence.

Example:

<u>S V V</u>   My older <u>brother</u> <u>goes</u> to college and <u>works</u> part-time.

            1. _____

            2. _____

            3. _____

            4. _____

            5. _____

            6. _____

Connecting Words: and, or

Often you need to connect words or groups of words in a sentence. One way to do this is to use a connecting word. Connecting words are called **conjunctions.**

There are many conjunctions in English. Two of the most common ones are ***and*** and ***or.*** They have different meanings.

    and joins two or more similar things in positive sentences

        I like Chinese and Italian food.

        Swimming and waterskiing are my favorite summer activities.

        We have class on Mondays, Wednesdays, and Fridays.

    or connects two or more similar things in negative sentences

        I don't like British or American food.

        We don't have class on Tuesdays or Thursdays.

        I can't play tennis, ride a horse, or roller skate very well.

    or also connects two or more choices or alternatives

        I would like to go to Hawaii, Tahiti, or Fiji on my next vacation.
        (I cannot go to all three places. I will choose one.)

My father or my mother will meet me at the airport.
(This sentence means that only one person will come to the airport.
Compare: *My father and my mother will meet me at the airport.* This
sentence means that two people will come to the airport.)

Use this chart to help you remember the meanings of *and* and *or*.

+ +		***and*** joins two or more positives I love tacos, pizza, and egg rolls.
– –		***or*** joins two or more negatives I don't like hot dogs or hamburgers.
T? F?		***or*** also connects choices Is this sentence true or false?

PRACTICE:

Using and, or

Work with a partner. Combine the two sentences in each pair to make one
sentence. Use *and* or *or* according to the meaning. Try not to repeat any
words.

Example: I like chocolate ice cream. I like coffee ice cream.

I like chocolate and coffee ice cream.

1. I can speak English. I can understand English. _____

   _____

2. I can't speak Tagalog. I can't speak Vietnamese. _____

   _____

3. Blue is my favorite color. Yellow is my favorite color. *(Be sure to make*

   the verb and the word color *plural.)* _____

   _____

4. Would you like soup? Would you like salad? *(You can have only one.)*

   _____

5. You can have rice with your meal. You can have potatoes with your

   meal. *(You can have only one.)* _____

   _____

(continued on the next page)

6. Helen Keller, a famous American woman, was blind. Helen Keller, a famous American woman, was deaf. _____

_____

7. She could not see. She could not hear._____

_____

Sentence Combining

Sentence combining is an exercise to improve your sentence-writing skills. When you do an exercise like the following, you combine several short sentences into one longer sentence. All the long sentences together make a paragraph. Your final product should be a paragraph.

There may be several correct ways to combine the sentences. However, there are a few rules to follow.

1. Don't repeat words if possible. For example, in the first sentence below, don't repeat *I am a*. You may omit words, but don't omit any important information.

2. You may change words. For example, you may change a noun to a pronoun or make a singular word plural.

3. You may add words. For example, in the second sentence below, you need to add the connecting word *and*.

Your goal is to write a smooth, grammatically correct sentence that contains all the information but does not repeat any of it.

Example:

    1. a. I am a figure.
       b. I am famous.

    2. a. I have white hair.
       b. I have a long white beard.

   I am a famous figure. I have white hair and a long white beard.

I am a figure and I am famous is a grammatically correct sentence, but a native speaker would not write it because a native speaker would not repeat the words *I am a.*

Another possible sentence is *I am a figure who is famous,* but this sentence contains unnecessary words.

You must keep the word *white* in the expression *long white beard* because it is important information.

WRITING PRACTICE 3 *Sentence Combining*

Work with a partner.

1. Combine the sentences in each group to make one sentence. There may be more than one possible correct way to combine each group.

2. Then write your new sentences in paragraph form. Do not number the sentences, and do not write them in a list. Write them as a paragraph.

WHO AM I?

1. a. I am a figure.
b. I am famous.

2. a. I have white hair.
b. I have a long white beard.

3. a. I always wear a suit.
b. The suit is red.

4. a. Adults like me.
b. Children like me.

5. a. Every year I take a trip.
b. The trip is long.
c. I do this on a special night.

6. a. I travel in a sleigh.[1]
b. The sleigh is magic.

7. a. The sleigh doesn't have wings.
b. The sleigh doesn't have an engine.

8. a. It is pulled through the night sky.
b. It is pulled by reindeer.
c. There are eight reindeer.

9. a. I fly all over the world.
b. I visit houses where children live.

10. a. I know if the children have been good during the year.
b. I know if the children have been bad during the year.

11. a. I bring candy and toys to the good children.
b. I bring pieces of coal to the bad children.

12. I am _____.

---

[1] **sleigh:** a kind of cart pulled by animals on snow

PART 4 The Writing Process

In this section, you will write a paragraph about your family. First, answer these questions to see if you have learned the main points of Unit 1.

REVIEW QUESTIONS

1. Organization
- What does a paragraph look like?
- What is indenting?
- What are margins?
- What is a title, and where do you write it?
- What should you do when a word is too long to fit at the end of a line?

2. Grammar and Mechanics
- What is a sentence?
- What is a subject? What is a verb?
- What are the three punctuation marks that you can use at the end of a sentence? When do you use each of them?
- What are five rules for capitalizing words in English?

3. Sentence Structure
- What is a simple sentence?
- What are four simple sentence formulas?
- What kind of ideas do you connect with *and* ?
- When do you use *or* ? (Give two answers.)

Freewriting

Freewriting is a way to get ideas. When you freewrite, you choose a topic, and then you sit down and write whatever sentences come into your mind about the topic. Don't worry about grammar, spelling, or punctuation, and don't worry about putting the ideas in order. You don't even have to write complete sentences. Just write everything that comes into your mind about your topic. If you can't think of an English word, write it in your own language. The goal is to keep writing for about ten minutes without stopping. Write horizontally across the paper as you do when you write a letter or a formal paragraph.

Here is an example of freewriting:

Freewriting about my Grandmother

I remember my grandmother. She was a great cook. The best cook. Every Sunday we had a big dinner. Fried chicken, mashed potatoes, green beans, and apple pie. Every Sunday we ate the same thing. We never got tired of it. It was our favorite. She never got mad at us. She always defended us when we got into trouble with our parents. When I picked all of the roses in her garden, she wasn't even mad then. My mother was really mad. Grandmother was kind and generous. She gave food to poor people. She never made them feel bad about taking it. She made people feel good. Just like she made me feel good when I picked her roses. She thanked me for picking her a beautiful bouquet. My mother was really angry, but my grandmother was always forgiving. Forgiving heart.

After you have written for about ten minutes, read what you have written and look for ideas that you can use in your paragraph. Cross out ideas that you won't use. Circle ideas that you can use. In the example on the next page, the student decided to write about her grandmother's kindness and forgiving heart. She crossed out the parts about cooking and food. She circled the ideas that seemed useful.

Freewriting about my Grandmother

I remember my grandmother. ~~She was a great cook. The best~~ cook.

Every Sunday ~~we~~ had a big dinner. ~~Fried chicken, mashed potatoes,~~

~~green beans, and apple pie.~~ Every Sunday ~~we ate the~~ same thing. We

never ~~got tired~~ of it. It was ~~our favorite.~~ *She never got mad at us.* She

always defended us when we got into trouble with our parents. When I

picked all of the roses in her garden, she wasn't even mad then. My

mother was really mad. *Grandmother was kind and generous.* She

gave food to poor people. She never made them feel bad about taking

it. *She made people feel good.* Just like she *made me feel good when I*

picked her roses. She thanked me for picking her a beautiful bouquet.

My mother was really angry, but *my grandmother was always*

forgiving. *Forgiving heart.*

Introducing Your Family

Work by yourself.

Write a paragraph about your family or about one person in your family. Use the paragraph "My Grandfather" (page 19) as a model. Practice everything you have learned in this unit.

Use these steps: gather ideas by freewriting, write the first draft, edit your work, and write the final draft to hand in.

STEP 1:
Prewrite to Get Ideas

Freewrite about your family or about one person in your family for about ten minutes.

STEP 2:
Write the First Draft

Now write the paragraph. Begin it with a sentence that describes your family (or a family member) in general. For example, *My grandfather is old in years but young in spirit,* or *My family is small and close,* or *My brother is the irresponsible one in our family.*

Then write ten to fifteen sentences about your family or family member.

If you wish, end your paragraph with a sentence or two that tell how you feel about your family or family member. For example, *We may live far from each other, but we will always feel close in our hearts,* or *My grandfather will always be young to me,* or *My brother will never grow up.*

STEP 3:
Edit the First Draft

Use the editing steps from pages 16–17. First, edit your own paper. Then ask a classmate to edit it also. Use the Paragraph Checklist.

PARAGRAPH CHECKLIST

FORM

☑ ☑   Check the paragraph form. (Does the paragraph look like the model on page 4?)

GRAMMAR AND MECHANICS

☐ ☐   Check for capital letters.

☐ ☐   Check the spelling.

☐ ☐   Is there a period at the end of all sentences?

SENTENCE STRUCTURE

☐ ☐   Check the sentences. Do they have at least one subject and one verb, and do they express a complete thought?

STEP 4:
Write the Final Draft

Write a neat final draft of your paragraph to hand in to the teacher.

ADDITIONAL WRITING

1. Rewrite the paragraph on page 12 about Mickey Mouse to be in the third person. Change the word *I* to *he,* and the word *my* to *his.* Begin like this:

   I would like to tell you about Mickey Mouse. He lives in a place called Disneyland. . . .

(continued on the next page)

2. Write a "Who am I?" paragraph. Choose a well-known person and give facts about his or her life. Give enough facts so that your teacher or your classmates can guess who your mystery person is. Write your paragraph in the first person. That is, use the words *I, me,* and *my.*

   Example:

   > I am a well-known athlete. I play on the Chicago Bulls basketball team. I am about six feet nine inches tall....

3. Write a paragraph about your best friend.

4. Write a paragraph about what you have learned in Unit 1.

Unit 2 Writing Instructions

ORGANIZATION

- *Time-Order Paragraphs*
- *Time-Order Transition Signals*

SENTENCE STRUCTURE

- *Compound Sentences*
- *Comma Splices*

GRAMMAR AND MECHANICS

- *Capitalization: Five More Rules*
- *Commas: Three Rules*

THE WRITING PROCESS

- *Brainstorming/Listing*
- *Outlining*

Prewriting: Brainstorming

Brainstorming is another method for getting ideas. When you brainstorm, you quickly make a list of every word, every phrase, every idea that comes into your mind about your topic. Write every thought down. Don't worry if it is correct or not. Your goal is to list as much as possible as quickly as possible.

Brainstorming is different from freewriting. In freewriting, you write words, phrases, and whole sentences across the paper horizontally. In brainstorming, you list single words or phrases vertically (from the top of the page to the bottom). You don't take the time to write whole sentences.

ACTIVITY:
Brainstorming

Work with a group of at least three students.

1. First look at the picture of the messy house after a party on the previous page.

2. Make a list of all the things you should do to clean it up. Write down every idea. Don't worry about putting the ideas in order. You will do that later.

3. After your group has finished brainstorming, your teacher may ask you to share your list with other groups. Keep your list. You will use it later to write a paragraph.

BRAINSTORMING LIST

_____

_____

_____

_____

_____

_____

_____

_____

_____

_____

PART *1* Organization

In this unit, you will learn to write clear instructions. That is, you will explain how to do something or how to make something—how to get to your house, how to cook a special dish, how to change a tire, or how to give a manicure, for example. You will do this in a time order paragraph. That is, you will explain each step in your instructions in order by time, and you will use special time-order transition signals to show the order. These are the two keys to writing clear instructions.

Time-Order Paragraphs

A **time-order paragraph** is a paragraph in which the ideas are put in order by time. For example, when you write about an event, you use time order to tell about it. You write *first this happened, next that happened, and then something else happened.*

When you write instructions, you use time order. You divide your instructions into a series of steps, and list the steps in order by time. For example, when you teach someone how to jump-start a car, you explain how to connect the jumper cables before you tell how to start the engine. If you teach someone how to make a cake, you tell how to mix the ingredients before you explain how to bake the cake.

As you read the model paragraph on the next page, notice that the steps are given in order by time. Also notice the time words that show what happens first, second, third, and so forth.

How to Have a Successful Garage Sale

It's easy to have a successful garage sale if you prepare for it ahead of time. First, collect used items in good condition. These items can be clothes, toys, books, dishes, lamps, furniture, TVs, pictures, and sporting goods. Clean everything well and store it in your garage until the day of the sale. Next, decide on a day and time for your sale. Third, decide on the prices, and mark a price on each item. If you are not sure how much to charge, check the prices at other garage sales in your community. Fourth, make signs advertising the date, time, and address of your sale, and put them up around your neighborhood. Then get some change from the bank. Get at least twenty dollars in one-dollar bills, a roll of quarters, and a roll of dimes. Finally, get up early on the morning of the sale, and arrange the items on tables in your driveway and in your garage. After that, sit back and wait for your customers to arrive. Be prepared to bargain! That's part of the fun of having a garage sale.

Planning a Paragraph: Outlining

Before you write a paragraph, you should plan what you are going to write. Think of writing a paragraph like building a house. You would never start to build a house without a plan; similarly, you should never start to write a paragraph without one. A plan for a writing assignment is called an **outline.** An outline helps you organize your ideas and put them in logical order.

Here's how to make an outline. The first step is to get ideas by prewriting.

STEP 1:
Brainstorm to Get Ideas

On page 32, you learned that brainstorming is a method for getting ideas, and you brainstormed a list of things to do to clean up a house after a party. Here is the brainstorming list for the model paragraph on how to have a successful garage sale.

How to Have a Successful Garage Sale	
collect used things in good	people don't buy broken or dirty
condition	things
clothes	get change from the bank
toys	ask your friends to help
books	decide on the prices
old dishes	put a price on each item
store them in the garage	buy price tags
clean everything	make sure everything is clean
clean the garage	wash and iron the clothes
arrange items on tables	advertise
borrow tables	try to have it on a sunny day
make signs	decide on a day and time
put them around the	be prepared to bargain
neighborhood	

STEP 2:
Edit the Brainstorming List

The second step in making an outline is to edit the freewriting or brainstorming list. Decide what you want to include in your final paragraph and what you want to omit.
- Combine ideas that belong together.
- Cross out words that repeat the same ideas.
- Cross out ideas that are not directly related to the main idea.

See how the writer of the model paragraph on the next page edited his brainstorming list.

How to Have a Successful Garage Sale

collect used things in good condition	~~people don't buy broken or dirty things~~
clothes	get change from the bank
toys	~~ask your friends to help~~
books	decide on the prices
old dishes	put a price on each item
store them in the garage	~~buy price tags~~
clean everything	~~make sure everything is clean~~
~~clean the garage~~	~~wash and iron the clothes~~
arrange items on tables	~~advertise~~
~~borrow tables~~	~~try to have it on a sunny day~~
make signs	decide on a day and time
put them around the neighborhood	be prepared to bargain

PRACTICE:
Editing a Brainstorming List

Work by yourself, with a partner, or with a group.

1. Turn back to your brainstorming list on page 32 on cleaning up after a party.

2. Edit the list.
   - Combine related ideas.
   - Cross out repeated ideas.
   - Cross out unimportant ideas.

3. Write your revised list on the next page.

REVISED LIST

_____

_____

_____

_____

_____

_____

_____

_____

_____

_____

STEP 3:
Organize the List

The third step is to put the list in order. To tell how to do or make something, the steps should be in time order. What happens first? Second? Third? Last? Notice that each step is given a capital letter (A, B, C, etc.).

LIST IN TIME ORDER

A. Collect used things in good condition

B. Clean the items and store them in the garage

C. Decide on a day and time for your sale

D. Decide on the prices and mark a price on each item

E. Make signs to advertise

F. Put signs around the neighborhood

G. Get change from a bank

H. Arrange items on tables in your driveway or yard

I. Be prepared to bargain

This list is almost a **time-order outline.** It just needs a title and a topic sentence to be complete. A *topic sentence* is a special sentence at the beginning of every paragraph that tells the reader what the topic of the paragraph is. You will learn more about topic sentences in Unit 4. Until then, we will suggest topic sentences for you.

To summarize, these are the steps in making an outline:

1. Brainstorm a list.
2. Edit the list.
   - Combine related ideas.
   - Cross out repeated ideas.
   - Cross out unnecessary ideas.
3. Organize the list.
   - Put the steps in order by time.
   - Give each step a capital letter.
4. Add a title and a topic sentence.

Here is the student's completed outline. Notice these points:
- The **title** is centered at the top.
- The **topic sentence** is below the title.
- The five **steps are listed** under the topic sentence and have capital letters A, B, C, and so on.

MODEL OUTLINE:
Time Order

Title:	How to Have a Successful Garage Sale
Topic Sentence:	It's easy to have a successful garage sale if you prepare for it ahead of time.

A. Collect used things in good condition

B. Clean the items and store them in the garage

C. Decide on a day and time for your sale

D. Decide on the prices and mark a price on each item

E. Make signs to advertise

F. Put signs around the neighborhood

G. Get change from a bank

H. Arrange items on tables in your driveway or yard

I. Be prepared to bargain

PRACTICE:
Making an Outline

Work by yourself, with a partner, or with a group. Turn back to your revised list on page 37 on cleaning up after a party.

1. Organize the list.
- Put the ideas in order by time.
- Give each idea a capital letter.

2. Look at the outline form below. Write the title on the top line in the center.

3. Read the topic sentence that is provided.

4. Write your steps below. (You may have more or fewer steps than in the form.)

Title: How to _____

Topic Sentence: Cleaning your house after a party is not fun, but it's easier if you do it step by step.

A. _____

B. _____

C. _____

D. _____

E. _____

F. _____

G. _____

_____

_____

_____

_____

_____

_____

Time-Order Transition Signals

A **transition signal** is a word or phrase that shows how one idea is related to another idea. When you see the word *finally,* you know that the last idea is coming. The phrase *for example* is also a transition signal. It shows that the next sentence is going to be an example of the idea before it.

In a paragraph giving instructions, you should use **time-order transition signals.** They tell your reader what to do first, second, and so on. It is important to use transition signals when you write instructions to make the order of the steps clear.

Time-order transition signals include the words and phrases in this chart:

TIME-ORDER TRANSITION SIGNALS

First, . . .	In the morning, . . .
First of all, . . .	In the afternoon, . . .
Second, . . .	In the evening, . . .
Third, . . .	At night, . . .
Next, . . .	
After that, . . .	Before an earthquake, . . .
Then . . .	During an earthquake, . . .
Finally, . . .	After an earthquake, . . .

Transition signals are usually placed at the beginning of a sentence. They are followed by a comma. *Then* is not followed by a comma; it is an exception.

PRACTICE: *Time-Order Transition Signals*

Work by yourself or with a partner.

A. Turn back to the model paragraph on page 34. Circle the time-order transition signals.

B. Each group of sentences below has a topic sentence (sentence 1) followed by several steps.

   1. First, number the steps in the correct time order.

   2. Then write two of the four groups of sentences as paragraphs.
- Copy the title in the middle of your paper.
- Copy the topic sentence. This will be the first sentence of the paragraph, so don't forget to indent it.

- Copy the remaining sentences in order.
- Add a time-order transition signal to some steps in each paragraph.

1. JET LAG[1]

_1_ Frequent flyers recommend these steps to prevent jet lag.

____ During the flight, don't drink alcohol or coffee.

_2_ Eat a high-carbohydrate meal before your flight.

____ Don't nap during the day when you arrive.

____ Go to bed early your first night in the new time zone.

Paragraph:

Jet Lag

Frequent flyers recommend these steps to prevent jet lag. First of all,

eat a high-carbohydrate meal before your flight. Second, . . .

2. HOW TO DRIVE YOUR TEACHER CRAZY

_1_ It's easy to drive your teacher crazy if you follow these simple directions.

____ Always come to class at least five minutes late.

____ Yawn and look at your watch as often as possible during the class.

____ Make a lot of noise when you enter the classroom.

____ At least five minutes before the end of class, slam your books shut and stare at the door.

(continued on the next page)

---

[1]**jet lag:** tiredness caused by travel through several time zones

3. **HOW TO TRAIN YOUR DOG**

<u>1</u>   Training your dog to sit and stay requires these five steps.

_____   Give the command "sit," and push down gently on the dog's back.

<u>2</u>   Put your dog on your left side, and hold the leash in your right hand.

_____   At the same time you are pushing down, pull up gently on the leash to keep the dog's head up. *(Don't add a transition word here.)*

_____   Return to the dog's side, and praise it generously.

_____   Remain at a distance for five seconds.

_____   Move one or two steps away from it, and give the command "sit-stay."

4. **HOW TO CHECK THE OIL**

<u>1</u>   Every driver should know how to check the oil in his or her car.

_____   Push the clean dipstick[1] all the way into its holder.

_____   Lift up the hood and lock it open.

_____   Add oil if the oil mark is below the "fill" line.

_____   Pull out the dipstick, and wipe it clean.

_____   Pull it out again, and check the oil mark.

_____   Replace the dipstick, and close the hood.

---

[1]**dipstick:** the long metal stick that shows the level of the engine oil

WRITING PRACTICE 1 *How to Clean Your House after a Party*

Work by yourself. Then work with a partner to edit each other's writing.

1. Write a paragraph titled How to Clean Your House after a Party. Follow the outline you developed on page 39.

2. Follow the same steps for writing and editing your paragraph as you followed in Unit 1 (pages 16–17). Use the Paragraph Checklist to check your work.

PARAGRAPH CHECKLIST

FORM

✔ ✔ Check the paragraph form. (Does the paragraph look like the model on page 4?)

ORGANIZATION

☐ ☐ Does the paragraph begin with a topic sentence?

☐ ☐ Are the steps in time order?

☐ ☐ Are there time-order transition signals?

GRAMMAR AND MECHANICS

☐ ☐ Check the capital letters.

☐ ☐ Check the spelling.

☐ ☐ Is there a period at the end of all the sentences?

SENTENCE STRUCTURE

☐ ☐ Check the sentences. Do they have at least one subject and one verb, and do they express a complete thought?

PART 2 Sentence Structure

Compound Sentences

In Unit 1, you learned to write simple sentences. However, if you write only simple sentences, your writing will seem choppy and childish. Using other kinds of sentences will make your writing seem more sophisticated and mature. One other kind of sentence is a **compound sentence.**

Remember that a simple sentence has only one SV combination. A compound sentence has two SV combinations joined by a comma and a coordinating conjunction.

> A **compound sentence** is two simple sentences connected by a comma and a coordinating conjunction.

Here is the formula for a compound sentence:

Simple sentence	,	COORDINATING CONJUNCTION	simple sentence

Notice that a compound sentence has a comma before the coordinating conjunction.

A **coordinating conjunction** is a type of connecting word. There are only seven coordinating conjunctions in English. In this unit, you will practice four of them: *and, but, or,* and *so.*

These are compound sentences:

Simple Sentence	Coordinating Conjunction	Simple Sentence
My family goes camping every summer,	**and**	we usually have fun.
Last year we went camping at Blue Lake,	**but**	we had a terrible time.
Next year we will take a cruise,	**or**	we may just stay at home.
We want to go to Hawaii soon,	**so**	we need to save money.

It is possible to connect three simple sentences. (Don't connect more than three, however, and don't use the same conjunction twice.)

Simple sentence, BUT	simple sentence, SO	simple sentence

We love to camp**, but** last year we didn't enjoy it**, so** this year we will do something different during our vacation.

~~We love to camp, **and** last year we had a good time, **and** we want to do it again this year, **but** we may go to Disney World instead.~~

Compound Sentences versus Simple Sentences with Compound Verbs

Caution: Do not confuse a compound sentence with a simple sentence that has a compound verb. Remember that a simple subject has only <u>one SV combination</u>. However, the subjects in a simple sentence can be compound *(My brother and I won)*. The verbs can also be compound *(We swam and fished)*. A compound sentence has <u>two SV combinations</u>. Compare the two pairs of sentences below. The first of each pair of sentences is simple and doesn't need a comma. The second one is compound and requires a comma.

Simple Sentence with Compound Verb:	<u>My family</u> <u>goes</u> camping every summer and usually <u>has</u> fun.	**SVV**
Compound Sentence:	<u>My family</u> <u>goes</u> camping every summer, and <u>we</u> usually <u>have</u> fun.	**SV, *and* SV**
Simple Sentence with Compound Verb:	Last year <u>we</u> <u>went</u> camping but <u>had</u> a terrible time.	**SVV**
Compound Sentence:	Last year <u>we</u> <u>went</u> camping, but <u>we</u> <u>had</u> a terrible time.	**SV, *but* SV**
Simple Sentence with Compound Verb:	Next year <u>we</u> <u>will take</u> a cruise or <u>go</u> to a Club Med.	**SVV**
Compound Sentence:	Next year <u>we</u> <u>will take</u> a cruise, or <u>we</u> <u>might go</u> to a Club Med.	**SV, *or* SV**

PRACTICE: *Simple versus Compound Sentences*

Work by yourself or with a partner. The sentences in this exercise explain some of the rules of American football.

1. Underline the subjects with one line and the verbs with two lines.

2. Write "simple" or "compound" in the space at the left of each sentence.

Example:

    simple   <u>One team</u> <u>kicks</u> the ball to the other team to start the game.

1. _____ The quarterback is the most important player on the team.

2. _____ The quarterback can throw the ball or run with it.

(continued on the next page)

3. _____ The quarterback can throw the ball, but the other players can only run with it.

4. _____ One team carries or throws the ball across the goal line of the other team to score a touchdown.

5. _____ Then the other team gets the ball, and it is their turn to try to make a touchdown.

6. _____ The offensive team can also kick the ball between the goal posts of the other team to score points.

7. _____ This play is called a "field goal."

8. _____ A touchdown is six points, and a field goal is three points.

9. _____ A football is oval in shape and is made from pigskin.

10. _____ Football players wear helmets on their heads and protect their shoulders with strong shoulder pads.

Coordinating Conjunctions: and, but, or, so

When they are used to form a compound sentence, the coordinating conjunctions have these meanings:

and connects two sentences with similar ideas; the sentences can be positive or negative.

My roommate is an art student, **and** her boyfriend plays in a rock band.

She doesn't like rock music, **and** he doesn't like art.

but connects two sentences with contrasting or opposite ideas.

She likes classical music, **but** she doesn't like rock.

She also likes country music, **but** he hates it.

or connects two sentences that express alternatives or choices.

Every Friday night, they go to a classical concert, **or** they visit an art gallery.

Then on Saturday night, he practices with his band, **or** they go to hear another rock group.

so connects a reason and a result

Reason	Result
They both like jazz,	**so** they go to jazz concerts together.
He works every night,	**so** they don't go out very often.
He can't practice at his apartment,	**so** he uses hers.

PRACTICE:
Simple versus Compound Sentences

Work by yourself or with a partner.

1. Analyze each sentence in the following paragraphs. Underline the subjects with one line and the verbs with two lines.

2. Write *simple* or *compound* in the numbered spaces.

3. Then write the formula for each sentence: SV, *(and)* SV OR SVV OR SSV, and so forth.

4. Add a comma to each compound sentence. Sentence number six is a command, so the subjects are not expressed. (You will need to add a total of five commas in the two paragraphs.)

How to Clear Your Ears in an Airplane

[1]Sometimes passengers' ears hurt in an airplane. [2]This pain can be quite strong. [3]It is caused by unequal air pressure outside and inside your ears. [4]The air pressure in the airplane may be at 15,000 feet but the air pressure inside your ears is still at ground level. [5]Airlines recommend the following techniques to stop the pain. [6]Pinch your nose closed with your fingers and pretend to blow your nose. [7]This action makes the pressure equal and usually stops the pain. [8]You can also yawn several times or you can swallow hard. [9]Children can chew gum and babies can suck on a bottle or a pacifier.

---

1. _____simple_____ _____SV_____   6. _____ _____

2. _____ _____   7. _____ _____

3. _____ _____   8. _____ _____

4. _____ _____   9. _____ _____

5. _____ _____

(continued on the next page)

How to Cure Hiccoughs

[10]My father has an interesting method of stopping hiccoughs. [11]First, he takes a glass and fills it with water. [12]The water can be warm or cold. [13]Next, he takes the glass in one hand and pinches his nose with the other hand. [14]Then he bends forward at his waist and drinks the water in very small sips from the opposite side of the glass. [15]This is a little difficult to do but it usually works.

10. _____ _____   13. _____ _____

11. _____ _____   14. _____ _____

12. _____ _____   15. _____ _____

PRACTICE:
Writing Compound Sentences

Work with a partner.

A. 1. Connect the two simple sentences in each pair to make a compound sentence. Connect them with *and, but, or,* or *so*—whichever best fits the meaning. (There may be more than one possible choice.)

2. Be sure to add commas.

Example:

Canada has two official languages. Government documents are printed in both English and French.

Canada has two official languages, so government documents are

printed in both English and French.

LANGUAGE FACTS

1. There are several hundred languages in the world. Not all of them have a written form.

_____

_____

2. Languages use symbols for sounds. They use symbols for ideas. (*Use* or.)

_____

_____

3. English uses sound symbols. Chinese uses idea symbols.

_____

_____

4. Chinese is spoken by more people. English is spoken in more countries.

_____

_____

5. Russian is the third most spoken language in the world. Spanish is the fourth.

_____

_____

6. There are about one million words in English. Most people only use about ten thousand of them.

_____

_____

7. Chinese has many different dialects. Chinese people cannot always understand each other.

_____

_____

8. French used to be the language of international diplomacy. Now English is used more often.

_____

_____

(continued on the next page)

9. International companies are growing. They will soon need more bilingual workers.

    _____

    _____

10. Young people should know a second language. They will be at a disadvantage in the international job market.

    _____

    _____

B. Make compound sentences by adding a SV combination to each of the following.

   Example:
   A good boss has a sense of humor, and <u>he (or she) is always fair</u> .

1. A good husband comes home from work in a cheerful mood, and

    _____.

2. A good wife has a part-time job, but _____

    _____.

3. An ideal teacher gives take-home tests, or _____

    _____.

4. Good parents want to raise healthy children, so _____

    _____.

C. Write compound sentences of your own. Use each of these coordinating conjunctions once: *and, but, or,* and *so.*

5. A good employee _____.

6. A good student _____.

7. An ideal roommate _____.

8. A best friend _____.

Comma Splices

One serious sentence error that writers sometimes make is called a **comma splice.** It happens when a comma instead of a period is put between two separate sentences. This mistake happens most often when the two sentences are related in meaning.

Comma splice: My uncle has his own business**,** he sells auto parts.

Comma splice: I was sick**,** I couldn't come to class yesterday.

In these two examples, two simple sentences are incorrectly joined by a comma. There are two ways to fix comma splices:

1. Change the comma to a period.

My uncle has his own business**.** He sells auto parts.

I was sick**.** I couldn't come to class yesterday.

2. Keep the comma and add a coordinating conjunction.

My uncle has his own business**, and** he sells auto parts.

I was sick**, so** I couldn't come to class yesterday.

PRACTICE:
Fixing Comma Splices

Work with a partner.

1. Find the comma splices in the following sentences. Mark an X next to these sentences. Some sentences are correct.

2. Correct the mistakes. Use both methods 1 and 2 above.

HOW TO HAVE A SAFE VACATION

Example:

____X____ Don't leave valuables in your hotel room, put them in the hotel safe.

Don't leave valuables in your hotel room. Put them in the hotel safe.

OR *Don't leave valuables in your hotel room, but put them in the hotel safe.*

_____ **1.** At airports and in hotels, watch your luggage at all times, don't let it out of your sight.

_____

OR _____

_____ **2.** Stay alert, and be aware of your surroundings.

_____

OR _____

(continued on the next page)

_____ **3.** Don't pick up hitchhikers, and don't stop to help someone in trouble.

_____

OR _____

_____ **4.** Don't stop when someone bumps your car from behind, drive to a police station.

_____

OR _____

_____ **5.** At night, park in a well-lighted place, and lock your car.

_____

OR _____

_____ **6.** Use traveler's checks, carry only a small amount of cash.

_____

OR _____

_____ **7.** At night, don't walk close to dark doorways, walk close to the street.

_____

OR _____

_____ **8.** Cross the street, join a group of people, or go into a store if you think someone is following you.

_____

OR _____

_____ **9.** At night, always go with a group, don't go into dangerous areas.

_____

OR _____

_____ **10.** Keep your car doors locked and your windows rolled up at all times.

_____

OR _____

WRITING PRACTICE *2* *Sentence Combining*

Work with a partner or by yourself.

1. Combine the sentences in each group to make one sentence. There may be more than one possible correct way to combine each group. Some of your new sentences will be simple, and some will be compound. For example, sentence 2 will be a compound sentence: *First, peel 6 apples, and cut them into slices.* Sentence 3 will be a simple sentence: *Don't make the slices too thin or too thick.* If you need to review the use of *and* and *or* to connect words and phrases, turn back to pages 20–21.

2. Write the fifteen sentences as a paragraph. Add time-order transition signals to some of the sentences. Don't start every sentence with a transition signal. Add them to sentences that give a major new step. Discuss and decide with your classmates which sentences give major new steps.

HOW TO MAKE AN APPLE PIE

1. Here's how to make a delicious apple pie for your family.

2. a. Peel 6 apples.
   b. Cut them into slices.

3. a. Don't make the slices too thin.
   b. Don't make the slices too thick.

4. a. Don't use apples that are sweet.
   b. Don't use apples that are soft.

5. a. Mix the apples with l cup of sugar.
   b. Mix the apples with ½ teaspoon of spice.

6. a. You can use cinnamon as a spice.
   b. You can use nutmeg as a spice. *(Choice)*

(continued on the next page)

7. a. Sift 2 cups of flour into a bowl.
   b. Sift ½ teaspoon of salt into a bowl.
   c. The bowl is large.

8. a. Add ⅔ cup of shortening.
   b. Cut it into the flour.
   c. Cut it with two knives.

9. a. Sprinkle ¼ cup of ice-cold water over the dough.
   b. Mix it in with a fork.

10. a. Shape half of the dough.
    b. Shape it into a ball.
    c. Flatten the ball.

11. a. Roll out the flattened ball into a circle.
    b. Don't roll it out too thinly.

12. a. Lay the rolled-out crust into a pie pan.
    b. Do this carefully.

13. a. Put the apples into the pie pan.
    b. Dot them with 2 tablespoons of butter.

14. a. Roll out the other half of the dough into a circle.
    b. Put it on top of the pie.

15. a. Bake the pie at 450° for 10 minutes.
    b. Bake the pie at 350° for 30 to 40 minutes longer.

16. a. Bake it until the top crust is brown.
    b. Don't let it get too brown.

PART 3 Grammar and Mechanics

Capitalization: Five More Rules

In Unit 1, you learned five rules for capitalizing words in English. Here are five additional rules.

RULES	EXAMPLES
Capitalize:	
6. Names of specific structures such as buildings, roads, and bridges	the **W**hite **H**ouse the **H**ilton **H**otel the **K**remlin **H**ighway 395 **S**tate **R**oute 15 the **G**olden **G**ate **B**ridge
7. Names of specific organizations such as businesses, schools, and clubs	**S**ears, **R**oebuck & **C**o. **S**pringfield **E**lementary **S**chool **C**ity **C**ollege of **N**ew **Y**ork **I**nternational **S**tudents' **C**lub
8. Names of the days, months, holidays, and special time periods	**M**onday **J**anuary **N**ew **Y**ear's **D**ay **R**amadan
BUT NOT the names of seasons	spring, summer, fall (autumn), winter
9. Geographic areas	the **M**iddle **E**ast the **S**outhwest **S**outheast **A**sia **E**astern **E**urope the **B**ay **A**rea
BUT NOT compass directions	Drive south for two miles and turn west.

(continued on the next page)

RULES	EXAMPLES

10. Titles of books, magazines, newspapers, movies, and TV series—also the titles of your own paragraphs

<u>Of Mice and Men</u>
<u>National Geographic</u>
<u>The New York Times</u>
<u>Raiders of the Lost Ark</u>
<u>Wheel of Fortune</u>
How to Tune a Car's Engine

NOTE 1: Do not capitalize all the words in titles. Capitalize only the first, last, and the important words. Articles *(a, an, the)*, conjunctions *(and, but, or)*, and short prepositions *(to, from, at, in, of)* are not capitalized.

NOTE 2: Underline titles of books, magazines, newspapers, movies, and TV series.

PRACTICE:
Capitalization

Work with a partner or a group. Write your own examples of Rules 6–10.

Rule 6

a building _____

a bridge _____

a road _____

Rule 7

a business _____

a school or college _____

a club _____

Rule 8

a day _____

a month _____

a holiday _____

a special time period _____

Rule 9

a geographic area
in your country _____

a geographic area
in another part of
the world _____

Rule 10 *(Don't forget the underlining rule.)*

a book _____

a magazine _____

a newspaper _____

a movie _____

a TV series _____

PRACTICE:
Capitalization

Work by yourself or with a partner. Change the small letters to capital letters wherever necessary in this letter from Heather to her friend Stacie.

> Aₐpril 23, 199_
>
> Dear Stacie,
>
>   I am so happy that you are coming to visit me this summer. I hope that you will be able to stay until july 4. We are
> 5 planning a big picnic on that day to celebrate america's independence day.
>
>   You asked for directions to my house from the airport, so here they are. First, pick up your rental car. I recommend hertz or avis. They are the biggest car rental companies here. Next,
> 10 drive out of the airport and turn north on u.s. highway 101. Go about one mile and take the first exit. Follow the signs to state

(continued on the next page)

highway 1, which soon becomes nineteenth avenue. You will pass san francisco state university, shriner's hospital, and a large shopping center. Continue on nineteenth avenue through golden gate

15 park. Then you will come to a bridge. This is the famous golden gate bridge. Drive across it and continue north for about ten miles. You will pass the towns of sausalito, mill valley, and larkspur. In larkspur, take the sir francis drake boulevard exit from the freeway. Drive west for three blocks, and then turn left.

20 Pacific national bank is on the corner where you turn, and across the street is a shell gas station, a safeway grocery store, and another bank. You will be on elm avenue. Finally, go one block on elm and then turn right. My apartment is in the marina towers. The address is 155 hillside drive.

25   I look forward to seeing you. Be sure to bring warm clothes because it is cold in june and july in northern california. In fact, sometimes it is colder in the summer than it is in the fall.

Love,

Heather

Commas: Three Rules

There are many rules for using commas. You have already learned two of them:

> **1.** Put a comma after time-order transition expressions (except *then*).

First, put four cups of rice into a pan.

After that, fold the paper in half again.

Before an earthquake, collect emergency supplies.

> **2.** Use a comma after the first part of a compound sentence.

Children can chew gum, and babies can suck on a bottle or a pacifier.

You can swallow hard, or you can yawn several times.

Cook the steak over high heat for six minutes, but don't let it burn.

EXCEPTION: This comma may be omitted in very short compound sentences.

Dogs bark and cats meow.

Turn left and drive one block.

Here is a third comma rule:

> **3.** Use a comma to separate the items in a series. A series is three or more things. These may be words or phrases (groups of words).

One dog, one cat, two goldfish, a bird, and four humans live at our house.

Every morning I get up early, run a mile, take a shower, eat breakfast, feed my pets, and fight with my wife.

Turn left at the stoplight, go one block, and turn right.

Notice that there is always one less comma than there are items in a series. If there are four items, there are three commas; if there are five items, there are four commas, and so on.

NOTE: If there are three items in a series, some people omit the last comma. In this book, however, use all the commas because they make your meaning clearer.

I have visited many countries in Europe, Asia, and America.

Shopping, relaxing, and visiting friends are my favorite weekend activities.

REMEMBER: With only two items, you don't need any commas.

I have visited many countries in Europe and Asia.

Shopping and visiting friends are my favorite weekend activities.

Work by yourself or with a partner.

A. Add commas where necessary in the following paragraphs. Not all sentences need them.

My Brother, the Sports Fan

[1]My brother is a sports fan. [2]His favorite sports are golf tennis skiing and swimming. [3]He skis in the winter swims in the summer and plays golf during the spring summer and fall. [4]He also watches baseball and football games on TV. [5]His bedroom looks like a used sporting goods store. [6]There are skis tennis racquets golf clubs footballs basketballs baseballs tennis balls soccer balls a bicycle and weights. [7]You often can't see his bed his desk or sometimes even him.

How to Fail a Driving Test

[1]It's easy to fail a driving test if you really try. [2]First park your car so close to the next car that the examiner cannot get into your car to begin the test. [3]It also helps to have your two front wheels far up on the curb—blocking the sidewalk if possible. [4]Second back out of the parking space really fast. [5]After that try to hit something such as another car. [6]Don't stop or even slow down at stop signs but speed up to get through intersections quickly. [7]Fifth try

to make your tires squeal while turning corners. [8]Next look for an opportunity to turn the wrong way on a one-way street. [9]Entering a freeway in the wrong direction will cause you to fail immediately. [10]Finally don't stop for pedestrians in crosswalks but use your horn to frighten them out of your way. [11]Just one of these techniques will probably get you an F on a driving test and two or more certainly will.

B. Complete these sentences to practice the "items in a series" comma rule.

Example:
Write a sentence that tells three foods you like. (*Use* and *before the last item.*)

I like _Japanese sushi, Chinese potstickers, and Mexican tacos._

1. Write a sentence that tells three foods you don't like. (*Use* or *before the last item.*)

   I don't like _____.

2. Write a sentence that tells three places you might go on your honeymoon. (*Use* or *before the last item.*)

   On my honeymoon, I might go to _____

   _____.

3. What are six useful items to take on a hike? (*Use* and *before the last item.*)

   When you go on a hike, be sure to take _____

   _____.

(continued on the next page)

4. Name two animals that don't get along with each other. *(Use and.)*

_____ don't get along with each other.

5. Write a sentence that tells three things you do every morning. *(Use and.)*

Every morning I _____

_____ .

WRITING PRACTICE 3 *Directions to Your House*

Work by yourself. Then work with a partner, and edit each other's writing.

1. Write directions to your house from school.

2. Follow the same prewriting steps that you followed when you wrote about how to clean your house after a party.

STEP 1:
Prewrite to Get Ideas

- Brainstorm a list of all the steps in your instructions.

STEP 2:
Outline to Organize the Ideas

- Review the brainstorming list. Cross out repeated and irrelevant ideas.
- Put the list into order by time.
- Make an outline.
- Add a title and this topic sentence:

    Here is how to get to my house from school.

(Your outline should look like the model on page 38.)

STEP 3:
Write the First Draft

- Write the paragraph. Begin with your topic sentence, and add some time-order transition signals.
- Practice the capitalization rules. Include some names of streets, businesses, and buildings.

STEP 4:
Edit the First Draft

- Edit your paragraph with a partner as you have done before. Use the Paragraph Checklist.

PARAGRAPH CHECKLIST

FORM

✔ ✔ Check the paragraph form. (Does the paragraph look like the model on page 4?)

ORGANIZATION

☐ ☐ Does the paragraph begin with a topic sentence?

☐ ☐ Are the steps in time order?

☐ ☐ Are there time-order transition signals?

GRAMMAR AND MECHANICS

☐ ☐ Check for capital letters.

☐ ☐ Check the spelling.

☐ ☐ Check the commas.

☐ ☐ Is there a period at the end of all the sentences?

SENTENCE STRUCTURE

☐ ☐ Check the sentences. Do they have at least one subject and one verb, and do they express a complete thought?

☐ ☐ Does the paragraph contain both simple and compound sentences?

☐ ☐ Check for comma splices.

STEP 5:
Write the Final Draft

• Write a neat final draft of your paragraph to hand in to your teacher.

PART 4 The Writing Process

In this section, you will write a paragraph giving instructions how to do or make something. First, answer these questions to see if you have learned the main points of Unit 2.

REVIEW QUESTIONS

1. Organization
- What are the two keys to writing clear instructions?
- How do you make an outline?
- What is a topic sentence?
- What are some time-order transition signals?

2. Sentence Structure
- What is a compound sentence, and how is one punctuated?
- What are the meanings of *and, but, or,* and *so* in a compound sentence?
- What is a comma splice? What are two ways to correct a comma splice?

3. Grammar and Mechanics
- What are the five capitalization rules in Unit 2?
- What are the three comma rules in Unit 2?

 **WRITING PRACTICE 4** Work by yourself.

1. Choose one of the topics below and write a paragraph about it.

2. Follow the same prewriting steps that you followed when you wrote about how to clean up your house after a party.

TOPIC SUGGESTIONS

How to prepare for an earthquake

How to play any game

How to make _____

How to teach someone to swim

How to bargain in your country

How to buy a used car

How to live on a small budget	How to put a crying baby to sleep
How to clean a house efficiently	How to have a safe vacation
How to beat someone at _____ (tennis, golf, chess, poker, etc.)	How to get a driver's license
	How to quit smoking
How to meet people in a new place	How to impress a boy/girl on a first date
How to wrap and decorate a gift	
How to get an A in a class	How to get an F in a class
How to prepare for a job interview	

STEP 1:
Prewrite to Get Ideas

- Brainstorm a list of all the steps in your instructions.

STEP 2:
Outline to Organize the Ideas

- Review your brainstorming list. Cross out repeated and irrelevant ideas.
- Put the list into order by time.
- Make an outline.
- Add a title and a topic sentence. Use this as your topic sentence:

    It's easy to _____ if you follow these simple instructions.

(Your outline should look like the model on page 38.)

STEP 3:
Write the First Draft

- Write the paragraph. Begin with your topic sentence, and add some time-order transition signals. Make your paragraph look like the model on page 34.
- Use time order in your paragraph. Also, practice the capitalization rules. Include some names of streets, businesses, and buildings.

STEP 4:
Edit the First Draft

- Edit your paragraph with a partner as you have done before. Use the Paragraph Checklist on the next page.

PARAGRAPH CHECKLIST

FORM

✓ ✓   Check the paragraph form. (Does the paragraph look like the model on page 4?)

ORGANIZATION

☐ ☐   Does the paragraph begin with a topic sentence?

☐ ☐   Are the steps in time order?

☐ ☐   Are there time-order transition signals?

GRAMMAR AND MECHANICS

☐ ☐   Check for capital letters.

☐ ☐   Check the spelling.

☐ ☐   Check for commas.

☐ ☐   Is there a period at the end of all the sentences?

SENTENCE STRUCTURE

☐ ☐   Check the sentences. Do they have at least one subject and one verb, and express a complete thought?

☐ ☐   Does the paragraph contain both simple and compound sentences?

☐ ☐   Check for comma splices.

STEP 5:
Write the Final Draft

- Write a neat final draft of your paragraph to hand in to your teacher.

ADDITIONAL WRITING

1. Write a paragraph in which you explain how to make an outline. Refer to the outline in the box at the bottom of page 39. Use time order.
2. Write a paragraph in which you describe your morning or your evening routine. Use time order. Begin as follows:

   My morning routine never varies. First, I get up at . . .

   OR   When I get home from school (work) at night, I follow the same routine. First, I . . .

3. Write about a dramatic event in your life. This could be a bad experience such as a traffic accident or a happy experience such as the birth of a child. Use time order. Begin as follows:

   I'll never forget the day (my daughter was born, we left our home forever, I was in a car accident, I broke my leg, etc.).

4. Write a paragraph about what you have learned in Unit 2.

Unit 3 Describing

ORGANIZATION
- *Space-Order Paragraphs*
- *Specific Details*

GRAMMAR AND MECHANICS
- *Adjectives*
- *Prepositions*
- *Prepositional Phrases*

SENTENCE STRUCTURE
- *Prepositional Phrases in Space and Time Order*
- *Position of Prepositional Phrases*

THE WRITING PROCESS
- *Clustering*

Prewriting: Descriptive Details

In this unit, you will write descriptions. Descriptions are "word pictures." You tell how something looks, feels, smells, tastes, and sounds. You need to become a sharp observer and notice many small details so that you can write a good word picture.

ACTIVITY:
Looking for Descriptive Details

Work with a partner or small group.

1. Discuss each picture on the next pages with your partner or group. What kind of person do you think lives or works in each place?

2. What clues in each picture led you to your choice? Make a list of the clues next to each picture.

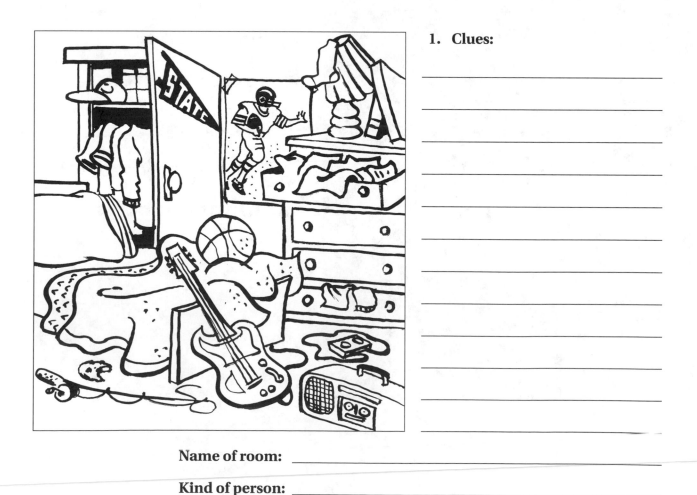

1. Clues:

_____

_____

_____

_____

_____

_____

_____

_____

_____

_____

_____

_____

Name of room: _____

Kind of person: _____

2. Clues:

_____

_____

_____

_____

_____

_____

_____

_____

_____

_____

Name of room: _____

Kind of person: _____

3. Clues:

_____

_____

_____

_____

_____

_____

_____

_____

_____

_____

_____

Name of room: _____

Kind of person: _____

PART *1* Organization

Descriptions

In this unit, you will learn to write good descriptions. When you write a description of a person, you tell what he or she looks like. When you describe a place, you tell what it looks like. If you describe a scene with people, you might first describe the place, and then you might also tell what is happening and what the people are doing.

There are two keys to writing good descriptions. The first key is to use space order, and the second key is to use specific details.

Space-Order Paragraphs

Just as you put the sentences in a time-order paragraph in a certain order, you must also put the sentences in a description in a certain order. Instead of using time order, however, you will use **space order.** In space order, you might describe something from top to bottom or from left to right. For example, when you describe a person, you could start with the person's head and end with the person's feet. You could describe a room from left to right or from right to left.

You might describe your classroom like this: Imagine that you are standing in the doorway. Write about each part of the room in order, moving from the left side of the room around to the right side and ending at the doorway again. When you describe a certain view, you might describe far-away objects first and close-up objects last. These are all ways to use space to put the sentences in a description into meaningful order.

top to bottom	bottom to top
right to left	left to right
far to near	near to far
outside to inside	inside to outside

Space Order

Work by yourself or with a partner.

1. Read the model paragraph, and decide which space order it uses from the list on the previous page.

2. Look at the paragraphs on pages 80 and 82, and tell which space order they use.

The Shared Refrigerator

My roommate and I share a refrigerator. My roommate's half of our refrigerator is very neat. On the top shelf is a carton of milk, a pitcher of orange juice, and a bottle of mineral water. These are arranged in a straight line on the shelf. On the next shelf are cans of soda. These are carefully lined up in rows. Orange soda is in the first row, Pepsi in the second, and 7-Up in the third. On the third shelf, he keeps dairy foods such as butter, cheese, eggs, and yogurt. On the bottom shelf sit plastic containers of left-overs.[1] These are neatly arranged by size. The large ones are in the back, and the small ones are in the front. There are two drawers in the bottom of the refrigerator. In his drawer, my roommate keeps vegetables and fruit. Each item is in a separate plastic bag in the drawer. My roommate is an organized person, and his half of our refrigerator really reflects his personality.

---

[1]**leftovers:** food that was not eaten at an earlier meal

PRACTICE:
Space Order—
Outlining

Work with a partner.

Analyze the organization of the model paragraph on the previous page and fill in the outline below. (For more practice in outlining, your teacher may ask you to outline the paragraphs on pages 80 and 82 also.)

The Shared Refrigerator

Topic Sentence: My roommate's half of our refrigerator is very neat.

   A.   On the top shelf _____

   B._____

   C._____

   D._____

   E._____

Concluding Sentence: My roommate is an organized person, and his half of our refrigerator really reflects his personality.

Specific Details

The second key to writing a good description is to use specific details. When you describe something, you paint a picture with words. Your goal is to make your reader "see" what you have described. The way to do this is to use a lot of **specific details**. *Specific* means exact, precise. The opposite of specific is *vague*. The more specific you can be, the better your reader can see what you are describing.

Here are some examples:

Vague	Specific
a lot of money	$500,000.00
a large house	a six-bedroom, four-bathroom house
a nice car	a Lexus
smokes a lot	smokes three packs of Camels a day
a pretty face	warm brown eyes, shining black hair, and sparkling white teeth

PRACTICE:	Work with a partner. Add as many specific details as you can to these vague

PRACTICE:
Being Specific

Work with a partner. Add as many specific details as you can to these vague descriptions. Then compare your details with those of other students.

Example:
My uncle is big.

A. _He is six feet, three inches tall and weighs 250 pounds._

B. _He wears size fifteen shoes._

C. _He can hold a basketball upside-down in one hand._

1. My boss has a nice house.

A. _____

B. _____

C. _____

D. _____

E. _____

2. My neighbor's children are spoiled brats.

A. _____

B. _____

C. _____

D. _____

E. _____

3. Carl is a bad driver.

A. _____

B. _____

C. _____

D. _____

E. _____

(continued on the next page)

4. The inside of the taxicab was dirty.

A. _____

B. _____

C. _____

D. _____

E. _____

5. The bus was crowded.

A. _____

B. _____

C. _____

D. _____

E. _____

WRITING PRACTICE *1* *Being Specific*

Work with a partner or a group.

1. Choose one person to be the secretary.

2. Rewrite the paragraph below to make the details more specific. Don't change the first sentence. Rewrite the other sentences, and write at least ten new sentences to add more details.

3. Check your paragraph against the Paragraph Checklist (on page 78).

The Limousine

The limousine was quite luxurious. It was big. The outside was nice. The inside was nice. It had nice seats. It had an entertainment center. It also had food and beverages. Our ride was fun.

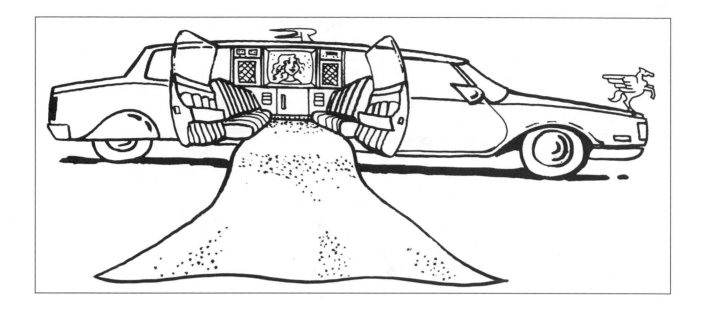

The Limousine

The limousine was quite luxurious. It was at least fifteen feet long. It had six doors and could carry eight passengers comfortably. The outside of the limousine . . .

_____

_____

_____

_____

_____

_____

_____

_____

_____

_____

PARAGRAPH CHECKLIST

FORM

☑ ☑   Check the paragraph form. (Does the paragraph look like the model on page 4?)

ORGANIZATION

☐ ☐   Does the paragraph begin with a topic sentence?

☐ ☐   Does the paragraph have specific details?

☐ ☐   Are the specific details in space order?

GRAMMAR AND MECHANICS

☐ ☐   Check the capital letters.

☐ ☐   Check the spelling.

☐ ☐   Check the commas.

☐ ☐   Is there a period at the end of all the sentences?

SENTENCE STRUCTURE

☐ ☐   Check the sentences. Do they have at least one subject and one verb, and do they express a complete thought?

☐ ☐   Does the paragraph contain both simple and compound sentences?

☐ ☐   Check for comma splices.

PART 2 Grammar and Mechanics

In this section, you will learn about two kinds of words that are very useful in writing descriptions. They are **adjectives** and **prepositions.**

Adjectives

Adjectives describe nouns and pronouns. Adjectives tell what things (or people) look like, what kind they are, or how many of them there are. Adjectives answer the questions *what kind? which one?* and *how many?*

what kind?	the <u>old</u> car with the <u>broken</u> window
which one?	the <u>fourth</u> chapter of the book
how many?	<u>twelve</u> students

Here are some things you should know about adjectives.

1. Adjectives always come in front of nouns, not after them.

<u>three</u> <u>young</u> <u>Japanese</u> <u>high</u> <u>school</u> students

2. Adjectives can also follow linking verbs.

be	He is <u>happy</u>.		**smell**	That smells <u>good</u>.
seem	You seem <u>sad</u>.		**taste**	Candy tastes <u>sweet</u>.
look	She looks <u>beautiful</u>.		**feel**	Silk feels <u>smooth</u>.

3. Adjectives are always singular. Never add an *-s* to an adjective or use a plural word as an adjective.

a six-foot wall	*(not a six-feet wall)*
a five-dollar bill	*(not a five-dollars bill)*
a two-year-old child	*(not a two-years-old child)*

4. Nouns can be adjectives.

the <u>English</u> book	a <u>shoe</u> store
some <u>tennis</u> balls	the <u>Japanese</u> students

5. Adjectives referring to nationalities and languages are capitalized.

an ancient <u>Egyptian</u> custom
my <u>Spanish</u> class
the <u>Cuban</u> government

6. *-ing* and *-ed* words (past participles) can be adjectives.

a <u>swimming</u> suit   the <u>bored</u> students
my <u>cooking</u> class   a <u>used</u> car
the <u>sleeping</u> baby   a <u>broken</u> heart
the <u>boring</u> class   the <u>stolen</u> money

PRACTICE:
*Identifying
Adjectives*

Work with a partner or by yourself.

1. Circle all the adjectives in the following paragraph. (Some sentences may not have any adjectives.)

2. Then draw an arrow to the noun each adjective describes.

My First Car

¹My first car was old and ugly, but I loved it anyway. ²The main paint color was black, but it also had blue, green, yellow, and white paint in different places. ³The body was in terrible condition. ⁴It had several big dents. ⁵The hood lock was broken, so I had to tie it down with a strong rope. ⁶Also, the back bumper was rusty, and the front window was cracked. ⁷The inside of the car was also a disaster. ⁸The inside door handle on the passenger side was missing, so you couldn't open the passenger door from the inside. ⁹The seats had at least ten holes in them. ¹⁰Also, the gas gauge was broken. ¹¹It always showed "full," so I often ran out of gas. ¹²The speedometer was broken too, so I never knew how fast I was driving. ¹³Like a first love, my old VW had a few faults, but to me it was perfect.

Prepositions

Another important kind of word is the preposition. Prepositions are little words such as *of, to, from, in, at, after, during, until.* Some prepositions are two words (*next to, because of, according to*) or even three words (*in front of*). Most prepositions are one word, however. Here is a list of common prepositions.

about	besides	near	under
above	between	of	until
across	beyond	off	upon
after	by	on	with
against	down	out	without
along	during	outside	according to
around	except	over	because of
at	for	since	in addition to
before	from	through	in back of
behind	in	throughout	in front of
below	inside	till	in place of
beneath	into	to	next to
beside	like	toward	out of

CAUTION: Some words such as *to* are sometimes prepositions and sometimes another part of speech. Compare these two sentences.

a. We went <u>to</u> the supermarket.
b. We wanted <u>to</u> buy some fruit.

In sentence **a**, *to* is a preposition because it is followed by a noun phrase (*the supermarket*). In sentence **b**, the word *to* is part of the infinitive verb phrase *to buy*.

Prepositional Phrases

A preposition is usually combined with a noun or noun phrase to make a **prepositional phrase** such as *at home* or *at six o'clock.*

Some prepositional phrases answer the question *where*. These are prepositional phrases of place:

at home	to the library
on the desk	opposite the door
next to the window	in my bedroom closet
under the bed	outside the garage
along the wall	between the two beds
in front of the house	around the corner

Some prepositional phrases answer the question *when*. These are prepositional phrases of time:

after class	in the morning
in 1999	at midnight
before a test	on New Year's Day

Other prepositional phrases show possession:

(the father) of the bride	(the colors) of the rainbow
(the name) of my boss	(the president) of the company

Others describe or identify someone or something:

(the woman) with red hair	(the man) in the dark blue suit
(the student) from Ecuador	(the car) with the broken window

PRACTICE:

Identifying Prepositional Phrases

Work with a partner.

1. Put parentheses ( ) around all prepositional phrases in the following paragraph. (One sentence has none.)

2. Underline the preposition in each phrase.

My Desk

[1]The inside (of my desk) looks like a second-hand store. [2]Each drawer is filled with junk. [3]In the center drawer, you can find paper clips, erasers, pencils, pens, rubber bands, and small bottles of glue. [4]I have a complete hardware store in my top drawer. [5]If you want to fix something, you can find whatever you need there. [6]In the second drawer from the top, I keep snacks in case I get hungry at night. [7]Small items of clothing are in the third drawer from the top. [8]The bottom drawer holds my collection of wind-up toys. [9]I play with them during study breaks. [10]I have such a variety of things in my desk that, according to my friends, I could start a small business.

WRITING PRACTICE 2 *Describing a Room*

Work by yourself. Then work with a partner to edit each other's paragraphs. Write a paragraph describing one of the pictures in the activity on pages 70–71.

STEP 1:
Write the Topic Sentence

Begin your paragraph with a sentence that names the place and tells what kind of person lives or works there. For example, your first sentence for the picture of the workshop might be one of these:

> This is the workshop of a very neat person.
> This garage belongs to a well-organized person.

STEP 2:
Write Specific Details

Next, write several specific details that describe the place. Suppose you had decided that the first picture is the room of a messy teenage boy. Write sentences that describe the mess. Use adjectives in your description.

STEP 3:
Write the Ending

If you wish, end your paragraph with a sentence that tells your feeling or opinion about the place. For example, you could write:

> I would make the owner of this room clean it up!
> The owner of this garage is probably a very good handyman.

STEP 4:
Edit the First Draft

Then edit your paragraph with a partner. Directions for editing are on pages 16–17. Use the Paragraph Checklist.

PARAGRAPH CHECKLIST

FORM

☑ ☑ Check the paragraph form. (Does the paragraph look like the model on page 4?)

ORGANIZATION

☐ ☐ Does the paragraph begin with a topic sentence?

☐ ☐ Does the paragraph have specific details?

☐ ☐ Are the specific details in space order?

(continued on the next page)

GRAMMAR AND MECHANICS

☐ ☐   Check for capital letters.

☐ ☐   Check the spelling.

☐ ☐   Check the commas.

☐ ☐   Is there a period at the end of all the sentences?

SENTENCE STRUCTURE

☐ ☐   Check the sentences. Do they have at least one subject and one verb, and do they express a complete thought?

☐ ☐   Does the paragraph contain both simple and compound sentences?

☐ ☐   Check for comma splices.

STEP 5:
Write the Final Draft

Write a neat final draft to hand in to your teacher.

PART 3 Sentence Structure

Prepositional Phrases in Space and Time Order

In Part 2 of this unit, you learned about prepositional phrases. Now you will learn how to use them in sentences to improve your writing style.

Prepositional phrases are used to show space order and time order. In a space-order paragraph, you can use prepositional phrases to show where the people or objects that you are describing are located: *on the left, on the top shelf, in the center drawer, next to the window.*

You can also use prepositional phrases in time-order paragraphs to show the order of events or steps: *at last, after an earthquake, during the war, until recently, before sunrise, at 12:00.*

Work with a partner or by yourself.

1. Turn back to page 73 and read the model paragraph "The Shared Refrigerator" again.

2. Put parentheses ( ) around the prepositional phrases of place.

Position of Prepositional Phrases

Prepositional phrases of time and place can be in different places in a sentence. They can be at the beginning, in the middle, and at the end of a sentence. Changing the location of a prepositional phrase can improve your writing. A paragraph can be boring if every sentence follows the same subject–verb–object pattern. If you sometimes begin a sentence with a prepositional phrase, your writing style will be more interesting.

Usual pattern:	The view from my bedroom window is especially beautiful in the fall.
New pattern:	In the fall, the view from my bedroom window is especially beautiful.
OR:	From my bedroom window, the view is especially beautiful in the fall.

Usual pattern:	Leaves of many colors litter the grass outside my window.
New pattern:	Outside my window, leaves of many colors litter the grass.

Moving a prepositional phrase is also possible in sentences containing *there is* or *there are*.

Usual pattern:	There is a large park next to my house.
New pattern:	Next to my house, there is a large park.

Usual pattern:	There are several kinds of trees in the park.
New pattern:	In the park, there are several kinds of trees.

Notice that you must put a comma after a prepositional phrase that comes at the beginning of a sentence.

Sometimes a prepositional phrase of place and the subject of the sentence can just exchange places. This happens when the sentence contains only a subject (S), a verb, and a prepositional phrase. In this case, don't use a comma.

Usual pattern:	S Two 14,000-foot mountains rise in the background.
New pattern:	S In the background rise two 14,000-foot mountains.

	S
Usual pattern:	<u>Soft white clouds</u> rest on the tops of the mountains.
	S
New pattern:	On the tops of the mountains rest <u>soft white clouds</u>.

You cannot move all prepositional phrases. You can only move those that tell a time or a location.

	I can't remember the name of our teacher.
Not possible:	~~Of our teacher, I can't remember the name.~~
	The man in the dark blue suit is a world-famous boxer.
Not possible:	~~In the dark blue suit, the man is a world-famous boxer.~~
Possible (time):	In the summer, the weather is hot and humid in my country.
Possible (location):	In my country, the weather is hot and humid in the summer.

PRACTICE:
Identifying and Punctuating Prepositional Phrases

Work with a partner.

1. Put parentheses ( ) around all prepositional phrases.

2. Put a comma after prepositional phrases of time and place that are in front of the subject of the sentence. Don't put a comma after those that are in front of the verb.

Example:
My favorite place (on the campus)(of our school) is the lawn (in front of the library.)(During my free periods), I like to go there to relax and talk (with friends.)

1. In the center of the lawn is a fountain.

2. Water splashes from the fountain onto some rocks around it.

3. The sound of the splashing water reminds me of a place in the mountains.

4. Near the fountain stands a group of tall redwood trees.

5. Under the trees there are wooden benches and tables.

6. On warm days students sit at the tables in the shade of the trees to eat their lunches.

7. The chatter of the students makes studying almost impossible.

8. After lunch it becomes quiet again in my special spot under the trees.

PRACTICE:
*Identifying and
Moving
Prepositional
Phrases*

A. Work with a partner.

1. Find and put parentheses around all prepositional phrases in the following sentences. Some sentences do not contain any.

2. Move one prepositional phrase of time or place to the front of each sentence.

3. Rewrite the sentence in the new pattern, and add commas where necessary.

Example:
There is a perfect place to spend a honeymoon (in Puerto Vallarta.)

In Puerto Vallarta, there is a perfect place to spend a honeymoon.

1. The Hotel Las Brisas has many small cottages, or little houses.

_____

2. There is a high wall around each cottage.

_____

3. A small, private swimming pool is inside the wall.

_____

4. Three rooms are inside each cottage: a bedroom, a bathroom, and a sitting room.

_____

5. There is also a sunny balcony outside the sitting room.

_____

6. The hotel staff bring you to your cottage upon your arrival.

_____

7. They leave you alone until your departure.

_____

8. There is no better place for romance and privacy than the Hotel Las Brisas.

_____

(continued on the next page)

B. Work by yourself or with a partner. Improve this paragraph by moving some of the prepositional phrases of place to the beginning of their sentences.

1. First, put parentheses around all prepositional phrases.

2. Then rewrite the paragraph. Move three or four of the prepositional phrases. Do not change every sentence. Change only a few of them in order to make the writing style more interesting.

The View from my Window

[1]The view from my bedroom window is especially beautiful in the fall. [2]Two 14,000-foot mountains rise in the background. Soft white clouds rest on the mountaintops. [3]A few apples still hang from the apple trees in the distant orchard, but the branches of the other fruit trees are bare. [4]The vegetable garden is next to the garage. [5]The last tomatoes of the year hang from their vines. [6]Fat orange pumpkins rest on the ground waiting to be picked to make Halloween jack-o'-lanterns.* [7]The leaves on the trees outside my window have turned a thousand different colors: red, orange, yellow, gold, rust, and purple. [8]Squirrels are making noise in the trees. [9]They are busy collecting food for the winter. [10]I enjoy the view from my window in every season of the year, but I especially enjoy it in the fall.

REVIEW QUESTIONS

1. Which sentences in the paragraph above are compound?

2. What kind of space order is used in this description?

top to bottom	bottom to top	right to left	left to right
outside to inside	inside to outside	far to near	near to far

---

*__Halloween jack-o'-lanterns:__ decorations made from pumpkins for the American celebration called Halloween (October 31). Faces are cut into empty pumpkins and candles are placed inside them. The lighted candles make the "faces" glow at night.

REVIEW PRACTICE:
Periods, Commas, and Capital Letters

Work with a partner. Add periods, commas, and capital letters to the following paragraphs.

Paragraph 1

> the neat desk
>
> my roommate's desk is completely neat her pens and pencils are lined up in straight rows and her pencils all have sharp points her paper clips rubber bands and erasers are in small drawers each drawer has a label on it on top of her desk there is a box with four shelves one shelf is for unpaid bills one is for paid bills one is for unanswered letters and one is for answered letters i sometimes think she spends more time keeping her desk neat than she spends doing her homework

Paragraph 2

> the messy desk
>
> the top of my desk is always a mess papers and books are lying everywhere at least five empty coca-cola cans are sitting on the desk broken pencils are scattered on top of it and on the floor under it the wastebasket next to my desk is full of used notebook paper empty potato chip bags and rotten banana peels eleven copies of <u>skin diving</u> magazine and nine copies of <u>computer world</u> are under the pile of books and papers you can't see the top of the desk because of the mess

WRITING PRACTICE 3 *Sentence Combining*

Work with a partner or by yourself.

1. Combine the sentences in each group to make one sentence. There may be more than one possible correct way to combine each group.

2. Write the sentences as a paragraph. Put prepositional phrases at the beginning of some sentences to show the space order.

THE SHARED REFRIGERATOR (continued)

1. a. My half of our refrigerator is messy.
  b. My half of our refrigerator is disorganized.

2. a. A box of eggs sits on the shelf.
  b. The eggs are broken.
  c. The shelf is the top one.

3. a. Carrots and salami share the shelf.
  b. The shelf is the second one.
  c. They share it with bread and lettuce.
  d. The carrots are limp.
  e. The salami is rock-hard.
  f. The bread is moldy.
  g. The bread is green.
  h. The lettuce is slimy.

4. a. Pizza lies under a bowl of spaghetti.
  b. The pizza is leftover.
  c. The spaghetti is three weeks old.
  d. These things lie on the third shelf.

5. a. The bottom drawer holds a combination.
  b. The combination is interesting.
  c. The combination is of paper bags of food.
  d. The food is from McDonald's.
  e. The food is from Taco Bell.
  f. The food is from the Chinese Kitchen.

6. a. A puddle covers the bottom.
  b. The puddle is disgusting.

7. a. My roommate and I are different.
  b. We get along.
  c. We do this very well.

PART 4 The Writing Process

In this section, you will write a space-order description of a place. First, answer the questions to see if you have learned the main points of Unit 3.

REVIEW QUESTIONS

1. Organization
- What are the two elements of a good description?
- What are some different kinds of space order?
- How can you make your details specific?

2. Grammar
- What is an adjective?
- Where are two places in a sentence that you can find adjectives?
- What is a prepositional phrase?

3. Sentence Structure
- What is special about prepositional phrases of place and time?
- How can you use them to improve your sentences?

Clustering

Clustering, like listing, is another way to get ideas to write about. You use the same brainstorming technique you have already learned. That is, you write down every word or phrase that pops into your mind about your topic. However, instead of writing them down in a list, you write them in circles, or bubbles, around your topic like this:

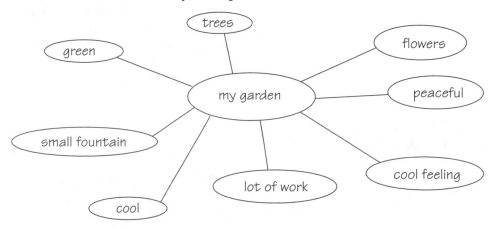

Next, think about the word or phrase in each bubble. Then write whatever comes into your mind in smaller bubbles. Also cross out any bubbles that you don't want.

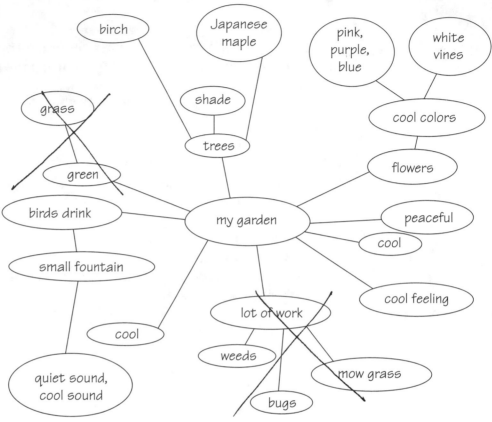

From these clusters or groups of bubbles, you can begin to see which ideas to use and which ones to throw away. Use the clusters that have the most bubbles, and throw away the ones that have few bubbles because they didn't produce many ideas.

You can also see that the word *cool* appears in several bubbles. This could be the main idea of the paragraph. The cluster *lot of work* produced several bubbles, but the idea of *cool* and *lot of work* are too different to write about in the same paragraph. Therefore, the writer crossed out the bubbles about work in order to concentrate on the idea of *cool*. The topic sentence might be: *Even on a hot summer day, my garden feels cool.*

WRITING PRACTICE 4   *Describing a Place*

Work first by yourself, and then with a partner to edit your paragraph. Write a paragraph in which you describe a place that is special to you, or choose one of the places listed below.

TOPIC SUGGESTIONS

Your classroom

The student cafeteria at lunchtime

Your grandmother's kitchen

A crowded bus on a hot day

The subway at rush hour

A disco on a weekend night

A beach at sunset

A holiday parade

Your house or apartment after a
  big party

A cemetery at midnight

Your workplace

A hospital emergency room

The town square on market day

The town square in a town in the
  evening

Follow these steps:

STEP 1:
Prewrite to Get Ideas

- Use the clustering technique shown on pages 91–92.

STEP 2:
Outline to Organize the Ideas

- The second step is to develop an outline. An outline from the clustering about "My Garden" might look like this:

My Garden

Topic Sentence: Even on a hot summer day, my garden feels cool.

   A. Flowers

      • cool colors (pink, purple, blue)

      • white vines

   B. Trees

      • cool shade

      • birch trees

      • Japanese maple trees

   C. Fountain

      • peaceful, quiet sound

Concluding Sentence: My garden's soft colors and quiet sounds make it a peaceful place to relax.

STEP 3:
*Revise the Outline
to Show Space
Order*

• In the next step, the writer changed the outline in order to use space
organization. She started with the flowers along the fence and moved to
the fountain in the corner of the fence and then to the trees around the
fountain. Since the white vines are not with the flowers but are in another
part of the garden (on the side of the garage), she put them last.

   Then she added the prepositional phrases of place to show the
space order. Her new outline might look like this:

My Garden

Topic Sentence: Even on a hot summer day, my garden feels cool.

A. Along the inside of the fence, flowers

- cool colors (pink, purple, blue)

B. In the corner of the fence, small fountain

- peaceful, quiet sound

C. Around the fountain, trees

- cool shade

- birch trees

- Japanese maple trees

D. On the side of the garage, white vines

Concluding Sentence: My garden's soft colors and quiet sounds make it a peaceful place to relax.

STEP 4:
Write the First Draft

- Begin your paragraph with a topic sentence that names the place and gives a main idea about it. Use an adjective such as *luxurious, messy, beautiful, plain, wild, mysterious,* or *ugly.* Your first sentence should be like these:

  The Club 100 is especially fun on Friday nights.
  Oceanside Beach is very peaceful at sunset.
  Our classroom is very functional.

- Use some kind of space order (right to left, top to bottom, far to near, etc.) Use prepositional phrases to show the order. Put some of the prepositional phrases at the beginning of their sentences.
- Write several sentences that give descriptive details. Be very specific. Try to paint a picture with words. You can describe objects, and you can also tell what people are doing in the place. Use adjectives in your descriptive details.

STEP 5:
Edit the First Draft

- Edit your paragraph with a partner using this Paragraph Checklist.

PARAGRAPH CHECKLIST

FORM

✔ ✔ Check the paragraph form. (Does the paragraph look like the model on page 4?)

ORGANIZATION

☐ ☐ Does the paragraph begin with a topic sentence?

☐ ☐ Did you use some kind of space order?

☐ ☐ Did you begin some of your sentences with prepositional phrases of place to show the space order?

GRAMMAR AND MECHANICS

☐ ☐ Check for capital letters.

☐ ☐ Check the spelling.

☐ ☐ Check the commas.

☐ ☐ Is there a period at the end of all the sentences?

☐ ☐ Did you use adjectives and prepositional phrases?

SENTENCE STRUCTURE

☐ ☐ Check the sentences. Do they have at least one subject and one verb, and do they express a complete thought?

☐ ☐ Does the paragraph contain both simple and compound sentences?

☐ ☐ Check for comma splices.

STEP 6:
Write the Final Draft

- Write a neat final draft to hand in to your teacher.

ADDITIONAL WRITING

1. Write a paragraph describing a favorite picture or photograph. Bring the picture to show the teacher.

2. Write one or more paragraphs of description based on one of the five Practice items on pages 75–76. Be sure to use space order to organize the specific details. Add more details if you wish.

3. Write a short paragraph describing a common object such as a pencil, a wristwatch, or a banana. Don't tell what it does. Just describe what it looks like. Don't use the name of the object in your paragraph. In other words, don't use the word *pencil* or *wristwatch*. Instead, use the word "whatsit" (= what is it?). Then read your paragraph to a classmate. Your classmate should be able to guess what you have described.

    Example:

    A whatsit looks like a long thin stick. It is about eight inches long, but it can be shorter. It is sometimes round on the outside, but it usually has six sides. It can be any color, but it is often yellow. One end of a whatsit is very pointed and sharp. The other end is soft and rubbery. What is it?

4. Write a paragraph about what you have learned in Unit 3.

Unit 4 Listing Characteristics

ORGANIZATION

- *The Topic Sentence*
- *The Supporting Sentences*

  Listing-Order Paragraphs
- *The Concluding Sentence*

SENTENCE STRUCTURE

- *Review of Simple and Compound Sentences*
- *Run-on Sentences*

GRAMMAR AND MECHANICS

- *Adverbs*

THE WRITING PROCESS

- *Detailed Outlining*

Prewriting

In the first three units of this book, you learned and practiced four different techniques for getting ideas: notetaking, freewriting, brainstorming, and clustering. You also learned how to make a simple outline. In this exercise, use the idea-gathering technique that you like best to develop material for a paragraph about animals. You may take notes from the class or small-group discussion. You may freewrite by yourself. You may find that brainstorming works best for you. Many people find that they get the most ideas by clustering. Use the technique that works the best for you personally.

ACTIVITY

Which animal do you think makes the best pet? Here are some possibilities.

| dogs | rabbits | chickens | turtles |
| cats | canaries | stuffed animals | snakes |

Discuss the topic with your whole class first, and then work by yourself or in small groups.

1. Discuss the animals on this list or other animals that are not listed. What characteristics of each animal makes it a good pet? Listed below are some possible characteristics. Ask your teacher to explain any new words or to tell you other words that you need. You may want to take notes during the discussion.

Adjective	Noun
gentle	gentleness
obedient	obedience
ferocious	ferocity
friendly	friendliness
aloof	aloofness
quiet	quietness
protective	protectiveness
dependable	dependability
intelligent	intelligence
loyal	loyalty
beautiful	beauty
independent	independence
self-sufficient	self-sufficiency
noisy	noisiness

2. After the discussion, choose one animal. Your choice may be serious or humorous. In the space below, freewrite, brainstorm, or cluster to develop your ideas.

3. Finally, complete the outline. In the blanks for characteristics, use either *all* adjectives or *all* nouns.

Outline

_____ are the best pets for _____ reasons.
(name of animal)   (number)

A. Characteristic _____

B. Characteristic _____

C. Characteristic _____

PART 1 Organization

The Three Parts of a Paragraph

A paragraph has three main parts. The first part is the **topic sentence.** It is called the topic sentence because it tells the topic or main idea of the paragraph. The second main part is the **supporting sentences.** The supporting sentences develop the topic. That means that they explain or prove the topic sentence. Some paragraphs also have a **concluding sentence.** The concluding sentence summarizes the paragraph and adds a final comment.

An English paragraph is like a sandwich. The topic and concluding sentences are the top and bottom pieces of bread, and the supporting sentences are the filling. The bread holds the sandwich together, and the supporting sentences are the meat and cheese.

When you write a paragraph, you first tell your reader in the topic sentence what you are going to say. Then you say it in the supporting sentences. Finally, you tell them what you said in the concluding sentence. This may seem clumsy and repetitious to you. However, clear academic writing in English requires all of these parts.

MODEL PARAGRAPH:
Listing Order

Goldfish

Goldfish make the best pets for three reasons. First of all, goldfish are very quiet. They don't bark, howl, meow, chirp, squawk, screech,[1] or race around the house at night while you and your neighbors are trying to sleep. Second, they are economical. You can buy a goldfish at your local pet store for about 50¢, and a small bowl for it costs less than $3.00. Water is practically free. Also, they eat only a pinch of dried fish food daily, so their food bill is quite low. Third, goldfish are very well behaved. They don't have teeth, so they can't chew your furniture or bite your guests. They don't ever go outside, so they can't dig holes in your garden. In addition, you don't have to spend hours teaching them commands such as "Sit!" or "Heel!" If you want a quiet and economical pet that doesn't cause any trouble, visit your nearest goldfish store.

QUESTIONS ABOUT THE MODEL

1. What is the title of this paragraph?
2. Which sentence is the topic sentence? What information does it give?
3. How many supporting sentences are there?
4. Does this paragraph have a concluding sentence? What is it?

---

[1] **bark, howl, meow, chirp,** etc.: different animal sounds

The Topic Sentence

The most important sentence in a paragraph is the **topic sentence.** It is called the topic sentence because it tells the reader what the topic of the paragraph is. In other words, it tells the reader what he or she is going to read. The topic sentence is usually the first sentence in a paragraph.

A topic sentence has two parts: a **topic** and a **controlling idea.** The topic part names the topic; it tells what the paragraph is about. The controlling idea part limits what the paragraph will say about the topic. It tells the reader: This paragraph will only discuss these things about this topic. For example, the topic of the model paragraph on page 103 is *goldfish.* What will the paragraph say about goldfish? The controlling idea tells us: *They are good pets for three reasons.* The controlling idea tells us the paragraph will not give us any information about the history of goldfish, how to take care of them, where to buy them, or the different kinds of goldfish. It will only give us three reasons they make good pets.

Usually, the topic comes first and the controlling idea comes second in the topic sentence. However, the controlling idea may come first. In the **a** sentences below, the topic is first. In the **b** sentences, the controlling idea is first.

	Topic	*Controlling Idea*
a.	Violence in American society has	several causes.

	Controlling Idea	*Topic*
b.	There are several causes of	violence in American society.

	Topic	*Controlling Idea*
a.	A good architect is both	an artist and a mathematician.

Controlling Idea
b. Artistic talent and mathematical ability are two qualities of
Topic
a good architect.

PRACTICE: Topic Sentences

The following paragraphs show how the controlling idea part of a topic sentence controls a paragraph. The topic of all three paragraphs is the same: *beaches.* However, the content of each paragraph is quite different because the controlling idea is different.

Work by yourself. Then check your answers with a partner.

1. Find the topic sentence in each paragraph.

2. Draw a circle around the topic and underline the controlling idea.

Example:

(Beaches) offer <u>different pleasures to different kinds of people.</u> Solitary[1] types can enjoy sunbathing or reading undisturbed. Social people can usually find someone to talk to or take a walk with. Curious individuals can collect seashells or study the habits of seashore creatures such as sandcrabs or sea-gulls. Athletes can swim, surf, jog, or play football or volleyball. Every type of person can find enjoyment at the beach.

Paragraph 1

Beaches

Beaches are fun in summer and in winter. In summer, you can swim and do many other water sports. If you don't like water sports, you can play beach games or relax on the warm sand. In winter, beaches are less crowded, so they are good places for solitary walks. Also, on a clear winter night, nothing is more fun than sitting with a group of friends around a big bonfire, talking, laughing, and singing. All year round, a beach is a place to have fun.

Paragraph 2

Beaches

Beaches differ in various parts of the world. Thailand has miles of empty beaches. They are beautiful, clean, and uncrowded, even in summer. You can spend the whole

(continued on the next page)

---

[1]**solitary:** alone; without companionship

afternoon on a beach and not see another person. In Japan, on the other hand, the beaches are very crowded. You can hardly find a place to sit down at the more popular Japanese beaches. The beaches in Northern Europe differ in another way. The water is cold, so most people go to the beach only to sunbathe. Along the French Riviera, the beaches are rocky, not sandy as they are on tropical islands. Each type of beach—empty or crowded, sandy or rocky—has its own special qualities to enjoy.

Paragraph 3

Beaches

People of all ages have fun at beaches. Young children love to splash in the water, jump in the waves, and play in the sand. They happily dig holes, fill buckets, and build sand castles all day long. Teenagers enjoy active water sports such as surfing, jet skiing, and boardsailing. They also like to just "hang out"[1] at the beach with their friends. Senior citizens[2] have a good time at the beach, too. They take long walks along the water's edge or simply relax and enjoy the sunshine. Indeed, children, teenagers, and even their grandparents can have fun at a beach.

---

[1]**hang out:** (*slang*) relax and socialize
[2]**senior citizens:** people older than about sixty-five

PRACTICE:
Topic Sentences

A. Work with a partner.

1. Circle the topic and underline the controlling idea in the topic sentences below.

2. Discuss with your partner what you think the supporting sentences could be.

Example:

(An ideal roommate) has three qualities.

1. Cigarette smoking damages a person's heart and lungs.

2. Cigarette smoking spoils a person's appearance.

3. Nonsmokers are also affected by cigarette smoking.

4. Hawaii is famous for its surfing beaches.

5. Hawaii has a perfect climate.

6. The "aloha spirit"[3] of Hawaii's people is well known.

7. An Olympic athlete must have talent and dedication.

8. College students take many kinds of tests.

9. Small cars are economical to buy, to operate, and to maintain.

10. Big cars are safer than small cars for two reasons.

11. A good boss has four important characteristics.

12. An employer looks for employees with certain qualities.

13. Living with an American family has three advantages for foreign students.

14. Attending a small college has several advantages for foreign students.

15. Students will have many different types of teachers during their school years.

---

[3]**aloha spirit:** friendliness to visitors

B. Work with a partner or in small groups. Add controlling ideas to these topics to make complete topic sentences.

Example:

Topic	Controlling Idea
Foreign students	often suffer culture shock.
Foreign students	are used to different teaching methods.
Foreign students	are interesting to have in class.

1. Our class _____

   _____

   Our class _____

   _____

   Our class _____

   _____

2. Foreign travel _____

   _____

   Foreign travel _____

   _____

   Foreign travel _____

   _____

3. Television _____

   _____

   Television _____

   _____

   Television _____

   _____

4. The English language _____

_____

The English language _____

_____

The English language __   _____

_____

The Supporting Sentences

The middle sentences of a paragraph are the supporting sentences. The supporting sentences support, or "prove," the idea in the topic sentence. In a listing type of paragraph, the supporting sentences are grouped under separate points. Each point is discussed in order. For example, in the model paragraph on page 103, the writer says that goldfish have three characteristics that make them good pets: they are quiet, economical, and well behaved. Then the writer discusses each characteristic in order. First, she says they are quiet, and then she writes one sentence about their quietness. Next, she says goldfish are economical and writes three sentences about costs. Finally, she says they are well behaved, and she writes three sentences about their good behavior.

Paragraph Unity

A paragraph must follow the rule of **unity.** _Unit_ means _one,_ so the rule of unity means that all the sentences are about one main idea. For example, if your paragraph is a description of your living room, you should write sentences only about your living room. Don't write about any other room in the house.

Another way of stating the rule of paragraph unity is to say that all the supporting sentences in a paragraph must be **relevant** to the main idea. That means that they are all directly related to the main idea. If they are not, they are **irrelevant.** For example, if your paragraph is about your mother's good cooking, a sentence such as _My sister is also a good cook_ is irrelevant because the paragraph is about your mother, not your sister. If your paragraph is about the harmful effects of smoking, a sentence such as _Many people smoke because it relaxes them_ would be irrelevant because it is not directly related to the main idea—that smoking is harmful.

When you write a paragraph, make sure that all of your supporting sentences are relevant to the main idea.

PRACTICE:
Paragraph Unity

Work with a partner or by yourself.

1. Read the following paragraphs and underline the topic sentence in each. Decide what the main idea of each one is.

2. In each paragraph, one or more sentences break the rule of unity. Find these irrelevant sentences and cross them out.

Paragraph 1:
Find one irrelevant sentence.

Christmas Morning

Christmas was my favorite holiday when I was a child, and Christmas morning was my favorite part of that special day. My brother and I usually woke up before dawn. We always tried to stay in bed until daylight, but it was hard. We usually got up while it was still dark and ran into the living room to see what Santa Claus had brought us. Then we raced into our parents' room and woke them up. Our father always grumbled[1] about the early hour, but he wasn't really angry. After our parents got up, we all went into the living room to open our presents. After that, we ate breakfast. We always had the same special breakfast on Christmas morning: blueberry pancakes, bacon, and hot chocolate. Mother makes a special breakfast on our birthdays, too. After breakfast, we played with our new toys. The gifts, the special breakfast, but mostly the family togetherness made Christmas morning a special time that I will always remember.

---

[1]**grumbled:** complained

Paragraph 2:
Find two irrelevant sentences.

A Dental Disneyland

Visiting my children's dentist is like visiting Disneyland. When you enter the office, Mickey and Minnie Mouse greet you at the door. The waiting room is full of activities for children. On the left, there is a round table that looks like a giant tooth. There are a lot of children's books on this table. On another table are Lego building blocks. In the middle, there is an area where young children can play with stuffed animals on the floor. On the right, there is a small room where older children can play video games. The dentist's name is Dr. Aubrey. He graduated from dental school five years ago. My children don't mind going to the dentist now because it is so much fun.

Paragraph 3:
Find two irrelevant sentences.

Nurses

A nurse should have at least five qualities. First, he or she must really like people because sick people are sometimes unpleasant and demanding. Second, a nurse must be organized. If a nurse forgets to give a patient his or her medicine on time, the consequences could be serious. Medicine is very expensive

(continued on the next page)

today. Third, a nurse must be calm. He or she may have to make a life-and-death decision in an emergency, and a calm person makes better decisions than an excitable one. Also, a calm nurse can soothe a patient who is upset. Doctors need to stay calm in emergencies, too. In addition, a nurse should be physically strong because nursing requires a lot of hard physical work. A nurse probably walks several miles during each eight-hour shift, and he or she often has to lift heavy patients into and out of bed. Finally, a nurse must be intelligent enough to learn subjects ranging from chemistry to psychology and to operate the complex machinery used in hospitals today. In brief, nursing is a profession for people who are caring, organized, calm, strong, and smart.

Listing-Order Paragraphs

In Unit 2 you learned how to write a paragraph using time order, and in Unit 3 you learned about space order. In this unit, you will learn about **listing order.**

In a listing-order paragraph, divide your topic into separate points. Discuss one point completely, and then another point, and then a third point, and so on. The order in which you discuss each point is your decision.

Listing-Order Transition Signals

Notice that in the model paragraph the writer introduces each of the three characteristics with a transition signal: *First of all, second,* and *third.* These transition signals are the same as time-order transitions. However, they don't show time order in this paragraph. Here, they are used to list the characteristics that are going to be discussed. For this reason, we can call these **listing-order transition signals.** *Also* and *in addition* are other listing transition signals. *Then* and *next* are used only for time order, not for listing order.

LISTING-ORDER TRANSITION SIGNALS

First, . . .	Second, . . .	Fourth, . . .	. . . also . . .
First of all, . . .	Third, . . .	Also, . . .	In addition, . . .

Place listing-order transition signals at the beginning of the sentence, and put a comma after them. *Also* may come at the end of a sentence with a comma or in the middle of a sentence without a comma.

> Also, they are good companions.
> They are good companions, also.
> They are also good companions.

PRACTICE:
Listing-Order Transition Signals

Work by yourself or with a partner.

A. Circle the listing-order transition signals in the model paragraph on page 103.

B. Read the paragraph about human intelligence that follows. Add listing-order transition signals in the blank spaces, and add commas where they are necessary.

Human Intelligence[1]

There are several kinds of intelligence. _____

there is mathematical-logical intelligence. People with this kind

of intelligence become mathematicians, scientists, or engineers.

_____ there is linguistic intelligence. People with

linguistic intelligence are good at language, so they become

poets and writers. We are familiar with these first two kinds of

intelligence, but five other kinds are not so familiar. There are

_____ spatial and musical kinds of intelligence.

Spatial intelligence is necessary for architects and artists, and

---

(continued on the next page)

[1]Based on Howard Gardner's *Frames of Mind: The Theory of Multiple Intelligences,* (New York: Basic Books, 1983).

musical intelligence is necessary for musicians. _____

there is bodily-kinesthetic intelligence. Athletes, actors, and

dancers have high bodily-kinesthetic intelligence. The last two

kinds of intelligence are interpersonal and intrapersonal.

People with these two kinds of personal intelligence manage

people well, so they become leaders of society. In short, there is

more than one way to be smart.

The Concluding Sentence

Paragraphs that stand alone (that is, which are not part of a longer composition) often have a concluding sentence at the end. A concluding sentence closes the paragraph so that the reader is not left expecting more.

Sometimes a concluding sentence reminds the reader of the main point by restating the topic sentence in different words:

> All year round, a beach is the place to have fun.

> In short, there is more than one way to be smart.

Sometimes a concluding sentence summarizes the main points briefly:

> If you want a quiet and economical pet that doesn't cause any trouble, visit your nearest goldfish store.

> In brief, nursing is a profession for people who are caring, organized, calm, strong, and smart.

Sometimes writers end a paragraph by making a personal comment:

> I never thought I would like cats, but our cat, Sally, has made me change my mind.

> With this information, I will never again feel stupid in my math class.

You may choose to use a conclusion transition signal to tell your reader that this is the end of your paragraph, or you may choose not to. Avoid the worn-out phrases *In conclusion* and *In summary*. Here are some other choices. If you use a conclusion signal, put a comma after it.

CONCLUSION SIGNALS

In short, . . .	In brief, . . .	Indeed, . . .

PRACTICE:
*Concluding
Sentences*

Work with a partner or by yourself. Write five concluding sentences for paragraphs based on the topic sentences in the practice on page 107. Use a concluding transition signal in some, but not all, of them.

Example:

Roommates will always have different habits and personalities, but

they can get along if they try.

1. _____

_____

2. _____

_____

3. _____

_____

4. _____

_____

5. _____

_____

**REVIEW
PRACTICE:**
Paragraph Order

Work with a partner. What kind of order does each of the paragraphs in the Paragraph Unity practice on pages 110–112 have? Choose from listing order, time order, and space order.

Paragraph 1, "Christmas Morning": _____

Paragraph 2, "A Dental Disneyland": _____

Paragraph 3, "Nurses": _____

Detailed Outlining

Until now, you have been making basic outlines using only capital letters next to the main supporting ideas. In this unit, you will begin to make more detailed outlines.

In an outline, you often have details that are not as important as a main supporting idea. These less-important details are set apart from the main points by giving them a number, not a capital letter. A more detailed outline might look like this:

MODEL:
Detailed Paragraph Outline

Detailed Outline

Topic Sentence: _____

  A. Main Point _____

     1. Detail _____

     2. Detail _____

  B. Main Point _____

     1. Detail _____

     2. Detail _____

     3. Detail _____

     4. Detail _____

  C. Main Point _____

     1. Detail _____

     2. Detail _____

     3. Detail _____

Concluding Sentence: _____

Of course, your outlines will probably not look exactly like this. There may be more or fewer main points and details.

PRACTICE:
Outlining

Work with a partner.

Make an outline of the model paragraph on page 103 by completing the form below. (For additional practice, make outlines for the other paragraphs in this unit.)

Goldfish

Topic Sentence: _____

_____

    A. *Goldfish are quiet.* _____

        1. _____

        2. _____

    B. _____

        1. _____

        2. _____

        3. *Water is practically free.* _____

        4. _____

    C. _____

        1. _____

        2. *They don't go outside—can't dig holes.* _____

        3. _____

Concluding Sentence: _____

_____

WRITING PRACTICE *1* *The Best Pet*

Write the first draft by yourself. Then edit it with your partner.

Write a paragraph called "The Best Pet" from the outline you wrote in the activity on pages 100–102. Use the model paragraph on page 103 as a guide.

STEP 1:
Brainstorm to Get Details

Look at your outline on page 102. Brainstorm some details for each of your three main points.

STEP 2:
Revise Your Outline

Then revise your outline. Add the details under each main point, and add a concluding sentence. Your outline should be similar to the model on page 117.

STEP 3:
Write the First Draft

Write the first draft. Be sure to use some listing-order transition signals in your paragraph.

STEP 4:
Edit the First Draft

Edit your paragraph with a partner as you have done in previous units. Use the Paragraph Checklist.

STEP 5:
Write the Final Draft

Write a neat final draft to hand in to your teacher.

PARAGRAPH CHECKLIST

FORM

 Check the paragraph form. (Does the paragraph look like the model on page 4?)

ORGANIZATION

☐ ☐ Does the paragraph begin with a topic sentence?

☐ ☐ Does the paragraph have a concluding sentence?

☐ ☐ Are the supporting sentences arranged in listing order? Are the main points introduced by listing-order transition signals?

☐ ☐ Is each main point supported by at least one specific detail?

☐ ☐ Does the paragraph have unity? (no irrelevant sentences)

GRAMMAR AND MECHANICS

☐ ☐   Check for capital letters.

☐ ☐   Check the spelling.

☐ ☐   Check the commas.

☐ ☐   Is there a period at the end of all the sentences?

SENTENCE STRUCTURE

☐ ☐   Check the sentences. Do they have at least one subject and one verb, and do they express a complete thought?

☐ ☐   Does the paragraph contain both simple and compound sentences?

☐ ☐   Check for comma splices.

PART 2 Sentence Structure

Review of Simple and Compound Sentences

Remember the formulas for simple and compound sentences:

Simple: SV

Compound: SV,   coordinating conjunction   SV

Remember that each SV combination can have a compound subject (SSV) or a compound verb (SVV).

Remember also the comma difference between a simple sentence with a compound verb and a compound sentence. A simple sentence has no comma before the coordinating conjunction, but a compound sentence does.

Simple sentence with a compound verb:
He works during the day and goes to school at night.

Compound sentence:
He works during the day, and he goes to school at night.

PRACTICE:
Review of Simple and Compound Sentences

Work with a partner.

A. Write S if the sentence is simple and C if the sentence is compound. Add commas where they are needed.

_____ **1.** The summers in the Midwest are hot and humid.

_____ **2.** Every evening it was too hot to sleep so my sisters and I played outside until after dark.

_____ **3.** Our parents sat on the front porch and watched us play our children's games.

_____ **4.** We played games such as hide-and-seek and tag or we just sat around and told stories.

_____ **5.** We also caught fireflies in glass jars and watched them shine in the dark like tiny flashlights.

_____ **6.** My sisters were afraid of most bugs but they loved to catch fire-flies.

_____ **7.** We usually had to go to bed at nine o'clock but on really warm evenings we could stay up until ten.

_____ **8.** Between nine and ten o'clock our mother or our father told us to come inside to get ready for bed.

_____ **9.** Sometimes it was still hot in our small bedroom so our parents let us sleep outside in the backyard.

_____ **10.** In those days, parents didn't worry about crime and no one locked their front doors at night.

B. Underline the compound sentences in the following paragraph. Add commas wherever they are needed.

Teenagers

Teenagers find many ways to drive their parents crazy. First they may dye their hair purple or they may shave their heads bald.[1] They may also shred their new sixty-dollar-designer jeans tattoo their skin or wear rings in their noses. In addition they spend hours at the shopping mall and on the phone. They have time to watch TV but they don't have time to do their homework. Also they're always too busy to clean their rooms but they're never too busy to "clean" the refrigerator by eating everything in it. Finally they are old enough to drive but too young to pay for gas. They are usually broke[2] so they always return the family car with an empty gas tank. It's hard to be teenager but it's even harder to be the parent of one.

Run-on Sentences

In Unit 2, you learned about errors called comma splices. Remember that a **comma splice** error is two sentences incorrectly joined by a comma alone.

Comma Splice: My roommate wants to look like Arnold Schwarzenegger, he spends hours in the gym lifting weights.

A similar error occurs when students write two sentences together with no punctuation at all. This is called a **run-on sentence.**

Run-on: My roommate wants to look like Arnold Schwarzenegger he spends hours in the gym lifting weights.

---

[1]**bald:** no hair at all

[2]**broke:** having no money

Comma splices and run-on sentences are especially easy mistakes to make when the second sentence begins with the transition words *then* and *also*. Be careful to use a coordinating conjunction when you use these two words.

Comma Splice: Small dogs don't need much space, also they don't eat a lot.

Run-on: We helped our hosts clean up after the party then we went home.

Fixing Comma Splices and Run-on Sentences

There are two ways to fix run-ons and comma splices.

1. Put a period between the two sentences, making two separate sentences:

My roommate wants to look like Arnold Schwarzenegger. He spends hours in the gym lifting weights.

Small dogs don't need much space. Also, they don't eat a lot.

We helped our hosts clean up after the party. Then we went home.

2. Make a compound sentence by adding a comma and a coordinating conjunction:

My roommate wants to look like Arnold Schwarzenegger, so he spends hours in the gym lifting weights.

Small dogs don't need much space, and they don't eat a lot. (Omit *also*.)

We helped our hosts clean up after the party, and then we went home.

PRACTICE: *Fixing Comma Splices and Run-ons*

Work with a partner.

1. Put an X in the space next to the sentences that are comma splices or run-ons.

2. Correct the sentences that you marked.

MORE ABOUT PETS

_____ **1.** Some people like cats, others prefer dogs.

_____

_____ **2.** Kittens are cute, also they like to play.

_____

_____ **3.** Dogs are good companions, and they can also protect you.

_____

_____ **4.** Dogs can bark at strangers they shouldn't bite them.

_____

_____ **5.** Lions are also good protectors, but they eat too much.

_____

_____ **6.** Penguins always wear tuxedos, they are good pets for people who like to go to fancy parties.

_____

_____ **7.** A pet elephant can fan you with his ears and spray you with his trunk, you won't need air-conditioning or a shower.

_____

_____ **8.** Goats cat lots of grass, so you will never have to mow your lawn.

_____

_____ **9.** A giraffe can reach things on high shelves, also it can see over the heads of people at parades.

_____

_____ **10.** Keep a boa constrictor[2] as a pet if you enjoy being alone then no one will ever visit you.

_____

WRITING PRACTICE *2* ## *Sentence Combining*

Work by yourself or with a partner.

 1. Combine the sentences in each group to make one sentence. Some of your sentences will be simple, and some will be compound. There may

_____

[1]**penguin:** a bird that lives in Antarctica. It stands upright and has black and white feathers.
[2]**boa constrictor:** a very large snake

be more than one possible correct way to combine each group. Do not change anything in the first sentence. Just copy it as it is.

2. Write the sentences as a paragraph. Add transition signals with each of the main points and with the concluding sentence. (Decide with your partner which sentences are main points. There are four main points.)

THE "WEAKER" SEX

1. Although it is often said that women are the weaker sex, women are actually superior to men in several ways. *(Don't change this sentence.)*

2. a. Women live longer than men.
   b. Women stay healthier than men.
   c. They do this in all countries of the world.

3. a. On the average, women live seven years longer than men.
   b. They do this in the United States.

4. a. This difference starts at birth.
   b. This difference continues until old age.

5. a. There are 105 boys to every 100 girls at birth.
   b. There are twice as many women as men at age 80.
   (Use but.)

6. a. Women are better than men at things.
   b. These things involve the five senses.
   (Change these things to that.)

7. a. Women have a sharper sense of taste.
   b. Women have a sharper sense of smell.
   c. Women hear better than men.

8. a. Men are physically stronger than women.
   b. Women are mentally stronger.

9. a. For example, more men than women had emotional problems.
   b. This happened in World War II.
   c. This happened during air raids.[1]
   d. This happened in London.

_____

[1]**air raids:** military attacks in which bombs are dropped from airplanes

10. Men are more self-destructive than women.
(Don't change this sentence.)

11. a. More men are murdered by other men.
  b. More men commit suicide.

12. a. Men drive more recklessly.
  b. Men have twice as many fatal accidents as women.
  (Use so.)

13. a. Do you still believe?
  b. Women are "the weaker sex."
  (Connect the two sentences with that. Do not use a comma. Your sentence will be a question, so put a question mark at the end.)

PART 3 Grammar and Mechanics

In Unit 3, you learned about adjectives and prepositional phrases. In this section, you will study adverbs.

Adverbs

The main job of an **adverb** is to modify a verb. Use an adverb when you want to tell more about an action. Adverbs answer the questions *how? when? where?* and *how often?*

how?	Drive <u>slowly</u> and <u>carefully</u>.
when?	Do it <u>later</u>.
where?	Play <u>outside</u>.
how often?	<u>Always</u> tell the truth.

Adverbs also describe adjectives and other adverbs. In this case, they answer the question *how?*

Describing an adjective:	I drive a <u>very</u> old car.	(*how old?*)
Describing another adverb:	Don't drive <u>too</u> slowly.	(*how slowly?*)

Formation of Adverbs

1. Most adverbs are made by adding -*ly* to an adjective.

Adjectives	Adverbs
slow	slowly
nice	nicely
beautiful	beautifully

Write two adjective–adverb pairs of your own:

Adjectives	Adverbs
_____	_____
_____	_____

2. A few -*ly* words are adjectives. There is no adverb form.

Adjectives	Adverbs
friendly	—
lonely	—

3. If a two-syllable adjective ends in -*y*, change the -*y* to *i* before adding -*ly*.

Adjectives	Adverbs
noisy	noisily
busy	busily

Add one adjective–adverb pair of your own like the examples.

Adjectives	Adverbs
_____	_____

BUT:

shy (one syllable)	shyly

4. Some adverbs do not end in *-ly*.

Adverbs of Time		**Adverbs of Place**	
often	then	here	inside
never	today	there	outside
now	yesterday	everywhere	upstairs

Add two examples of your own:

_____ _____

5. A few adverbs are irregular.

Adjectives	**Adverbs**	
good	well	*She's a good swimmer. She swims well.*
fast	fast	*He's a fast runner. He runs fast.*
hard	hard	*It was a hard test. The students worked hard.*

PRACTICE:
Identifying Adjectives and Adverbs

Work by yourself or with a partner.

A. 1. Underline all of the adjectives in the following paragraph. (There are eighteen adjectives in the six sentences.)

2. Be prepared to tell which word each adjective describes.

> [1]The <u>new</u> owner of the dry cleaner's near my house is very attractive. [2]She is slim and petite. [3]She has shining black hair, friendly brown eyes, and thick black eyelashes. [4]She greets her customers with a warm smile. [5]She says a few pleasant words to everyone who comes into her spotlessly clean shop. [6]She is also a hard worker, and I feel certain that she will be successful in her new business.

(continued on the next page)

B. **I.** Underline all of the adverbs in the following paragraph. (There are sixteen adverbs in the seven sentences. One sentence doesn't contain any.)

2. Be able to tell which word each adverb modifies.

3. Also tell what question it answers: *how, where, when,* or *how often.*

4. Finally, find the three adjectives in this paragraph.

[1]My roommate and I are <u>exactly</u> opposite, but we get along very well. [2]He walks, talks, eats, and works slowly, but I do everything quickly. [3]He gets up early, but I like to sleep late. [4]He does his homework eagerly, but I do mine unenthusiastically. [5]His room is very neat, but I leave my clothes and books everywhere. [6]He always drives cautiously and says that I often drive too fast. [7]In fact, he thinks that I am a reckless driver.

C. **I.** Tell whether the underlined words are adjectives or adverbs.

2. Draw an arrow to the word each one describes.

3. Be able to tell what question it answers.

Example:

adv. (where?)   adj. (which one?)
The students waited <u>outside</u> for someone to open the <u>locked</u> classroom.

1. The <u>sick</u> child sat <u>quietly</u> reading a <u>comic</u> book.

2. I am <u>very</u> <u>shy</u>, so I don't talk <u>easily</u> in front of strangers.

3. The <u>little</u> girl smiled <u>shyly</u> at her <u>new</u> friend.

4. The <u>barking</u> dog disturbed the neighborhood.

5. The <u>loudly</u> <u>barking</u> dog disturbed the <u>whole</u> neighborhood.

D. Choose the words from the list that fit the meaning of the sentence. Then write the correct form of the word (adjective or adverb) from each pair in the blanks.

noisy–noisily	polite–politely	angry–angrily
reckless–recklessly	joyous–joyously	

1. My teenage cousin is a _____ driver. He always drives

_____ , and last week he got a ticket.

2. The tourists listened _____ while the tour guide

explained the importance of the monument. One _____

tourist asked the guide to please speak louder.

3. The _____ crowd listened to the speech. Then they began

to shout and shake their fists _____ at the speaker. The

women in the audience were especially _____ because

the speaker had attacked women's rights.

4. The little children ran _____ downstairs to see what Santa

Claus had left for them under the Christmas tree. Christmas is one of

the most _____ holidays in the United States.

5. Last night, there was a _____ party in my apartment building.

People were singing and dancing _____ half the night while

I was trying to study.

E. For each pair of words, write two sentences of your own. In one sentence, use the adjective form. In the other sentence, use the adverb form.

dangerous–dangerously

1. _____

2. _____

rude–rudely

1. _____

2. _____

passionate–passionately

1. _____

2. _____

WRITING PRACTICE 3 *Describing with Adjectives and Adverbs*

Work by yourself. Write two short paragraphs about someone you know well. The purpose of this writing practice is to practice grammar. Therefore, do not worry about prewriting, paragraph organization, topic sentences, transition signals, and so on. Just concentrate on writing interesting sentences.

1. In the first paragraph, use adjectives to describe the person's appearance. Is he or she *tall, short, fat, thin,* or does he or she have a *medium* build? Does he or she have *blond, black, brown,* or *gray* hair? Is his or her complexion *light* or *dark?* What kind of clothes does he or she wear? Write five to eight sentences.

2. In the second paragraph, use adverbs to describe how the person acts. How does he or she speak? *(Softly? Loudly?)* How does he or she cook, drive, sing, dance, write, do homework? Does he or she make friends *easily?* Does he or she attend class *regularly?* Write five to eight sentences.

PART 4 The Writing Process

In this section, you will write a listing-order paragraph about a person. First, answer these questions to see if you have learned the main points of Unit 4.

REVIEW QUESTIONS

1. Organization
- What are the three parts of a paragraph?
- What are the two parts of a topic sentence?
- What does the controlling idea do?
- What is unity in a paragraph?
- What is listing order?
- What are some listing-order transition signals?
- How do you write a concluding sentence?

2. Sentence Structure
- What are two serious sentence errors?
- What are two ways to correct them?

3. Grammar and Mechanics
- What kinds of words do adverbs modify?
- What questions do they answer?

WRITING PRACTICE 4 *An Ideal Person*

Write about the qualities of an ideal roommate, boss, husband, wife, friend, teacher, student, politician, bank robber, soldier, prison guard, and so forth. Your paragraph may be serious or humorous. The paragraph about nurses on pages 111–112 is an example of a serious paragraph, and the paragraph about teenagers on page 121 is an example of a humorous paragraph.

First, brainstorm together with a classmate or a group to get ideas. Then work alone to develop an outline and to write the first draft. Finally, edit your paragraph with a classmate.

STEP 1: *Prewrite to Get Ideas*	Choose a type of person from the list above (or one of your own choosing). Then brainstorm for ideas by listing or clustering. If you are working alone, you may want to freewrite. Try to find three or four qualities and at least one detail for each quality.
STEP 2: *Outline to Organize the Ideas*	Then make an outline for your paragraph. Your outline should include a topic sentence, three or four main points, some details, and a concluding sentence. It should be similar to the model outline on page 116.
STEP 3: *Write the First Draft*	Write the first draft. Be sure to use some listing-order transition signals in your paragraph.
STEP 4: *Edit the First Draft*	Edit your paragraph with a partner as you have done in previous units. Use the Paragraph Checklist.
STEP 5: *Write the Final Draft*	Write a neat final draft to hand in to your teacher.

PARAGRAPH CHECKLIST

FORM

 Check the paragraph form. (Does the paragraph look like the model on page 4?)

ORGANIZATION

☐ ☐ Does the paragraph begin with a topic sentence?

☐ ☐ Does the paragraph have a concluding sentence?

☐ ☐ Are the supporting sentences arranged in listing order? Are the main points introduced by listing-order transition signals?

☐ ☐ Is each main point supported by at least one specific detail?

☐ ☐ Does the paragraph have unity? (no irrelevant sentences)

GRAMMAR AND MECHANICS

☐ ☐ Check for capital letters.

☐ ☐ Check the spelling.

☐ ☐ Check the commas.

☐ ☐ Is there a period at the end of all the sentences?

SENTENCE STRUCTURE

☐ ☐ Check the sentences. Do they have at least one subject and one verb, and do they express a complete thought?

☐ ☐ Does the paragraph contain both simple and compound sentences?

☐ ☐ Check for comma splices and run-ons.

ADDITIONAL WRITING

1. Write a paragraph about any of the topic sentences from the topic sentence practices on page 107.

2. Write a paragraph about the three kinds of paragraphs you have studied so far.

3. Write a paragraph about what you have learned in Unit 4.

Unit 5 Stating Reasons and Using Examples

ORGANIZATION

- *Reasons and Examples*
- *Transition Signals with Reasons and Examples*

SENTENCE STRUCTURE

- *Independent and Dependent Clauses*
- *Complex Sentences*
- *Fragments*

GRAMMAR AND MECHANICS

- *Commas: Four More Rules*
- *Capitalization: Two More Rules*
- *Personal Letter Form*

THE WRITING PROCESS

Prewriting

In this unit, you will write another listing-order paragraph and use reasons and specific examples to prove your points. Use whichever prewriting method works best for you to do the following activity.

ACTIVITY

Work with a partner or small group.

1. If you could go anywhere in the world, where would you like to go on your next vacation? Choose a place that everyone in your group knows well. It can be a city such as Paris or Hong Kong, a state such as Hawaii, or an entire country such as Costa Rica.

2. Think of at least three reasons for your choice (or more if you can). Here are some possible reasons.

climate	museums	architecture
tourist attractions	shopping	night life
scenery	friendly people	good restaurants
cultural life	beaches	costs

Use the space below to do your brainstorming or clustering.

3. Now do more brainstorming or clustering to find one <u>specific</u> example for each reason. A specific example might be the name of a tourist attraction (the Eiffel Tower in Paris), a beach (Waikiki Beach in Hawaii), or a store (Gucci). A specific example could also be a temperature (78°F) or a number (50 miles, $35.00 per night for a hotel room).

4. Complete the outline.

Outline

_____ is a great _____
(name of place)   *(city/state/country/area)*

to visit for several reasons.

    Reason A: _____

          Example: _____

    Reason B: _____

          Example: _____

    Reason C: _____

          Example: _____

    Reason D: _____

          Example: _____

PART **1** Organization

In this unit, you will learn to give reasons and use examples to support your reasons. Read the model paragraph below. Then answer the questions.

MODEL PARAGRAPH:
Using Examples

Costa Rica

Costa Rica is a great place to spend a vacation for two reasons. First of all, Costa Rica has an excellent system of national parks where visitors can observe nature. For example, in Tortuguero National Park, visitors can watch sea turtles come ashore[1] to lay their eggs in the sand. Then they can come back several months later to see the new babies crawl down to the sea. In Santa Rosa National Park, visitors can see unusual birds such as toucans and quetzals and exotic animals such as spider monkeys. Second, Costa Rica has many beautiful beaches. For instance, the beaches at Manuel Antonio National Park are among the most beautiful in the world, and the beaches on Cañoa and Cocos Islands offer perfect conditions for snorkeling and scuba diving. Indeed, Costa Rica is a wonderful place to go if you love the outdoors.

---

[1]**ashore:** on the shore, on the beach

QUESTIONS ABOUT THE MODEL

1. What is the title of this paragraph?

2. What is the topic sentence? What information does it give you?

3. How many supporting sentences are there?

4. How many reasons are given? What words introduce these reasons?

5. How many examples are given for each reason? What words tell you that these are examples?

6. What is the concluding sentence?

PRACTICE:
Outlining

Complete the outline of the model paragraph. Use another piece of paper if necessary.

_____ (Title)

Topic Sentence: _____

_____

Reason A: _____

    Example 1: _____

    Example 2: _____

Reason B: _____

    Example 1: _____

    Example 2: _____

Concluding Sentence: _____

_____

Reasons and Examples

When you write a topic sentence such as *Costa Rica is a great place to visit,* or *Women should not be jet fighter pilots,* you need to support it with **reasons.** You need to explain *why* Costa Rica is a great place to visit, or *why* women should not be jet fighter pilots. The writer of the model paragraph gave two main reasons why tourists enjoy visiting Costa Rica:

1. It has many national parks where tourists can see nature.

2. It has beautiful beaches.

After you state your reasons, you need to support them. A good way to support reasons is to give **specific examples.** Specific examples can be names of specific people (John Lennon), places (the lunchroom at your place of work), or things (a Honda Civic). Examples can also be specific numbers (25,000 people) or amounts of money ($5.23). Examples can be specific days such as Hanukkah, New Year's Day, or July 4. Examples can also be events from your personal experience.

In the model paragraph, each of the reasons has two supporting examples. The examples are specific. They are the actual names of places: Tortuguero National Park, Santa Rosa National Park, Manuel Antonio National Park, Cañoa Island, and Cocos Island. Other specific examples in the paragraph are the names of birds (toucans and quetzals) and of an animal (spider monkeys).

PRACTICE:
Specific Supporting Examples

Work with a partner. Think of at least one specific example for each reason in the following outlines. If you can, give two examples.

Outline A

Topic Sentence:	Small cars are more economical than big cars.
Reason:	A. They don't use much gasoline
Example:	1. A Honda Civic gets forty miles per gallon.
Example:	2. _____
Reason:	B. Maintenance costs are lower.
Example:	1. _____
Example:	2. _____
Reason:	C. Repair costs are lower.
Example:	1. _____
Example:	2. _____
Reason:	D. Insurance is cheaper.
Example:	1. _____
Example:	2. _____
Concluding Sentence:	You save money on gas, maintenance, repairs, and insurance when you own a small car.

Outline B

Topic Sentence: I chose this college for three reasons.

Reason: A. The location is convenient.

Example: 1. _____

Example: 2. _____

Reason: B. The classes are small.

Example: 1. _____

Example: 2. _____

Reason: C. The cost is affordable.

Example: 1. _____

Example: 2. _____

Concluding Sentence: I decided to attend the College of Marin because it is convenient, small, and affordable.

For the last two outlines, think of your own reasons.

Outline C

Topic Sentence: Sloppy Joe's is the worst (best) fast-food restaurant in town.

Reason: A. _____

Example: 1. _____

Example: 2. _____

Reason: B. _____

Example: 1. _____

Example: 2. _____

(continued on the next page)

Reason:	C. _____
Example:	1. _____
Example:	2. _____
Concluding Sentence:	Never (always) eat at Sloppy Joe's because it is _____ ,

_____ , and _____ .

Outline D

Topic Sentence:	My Uncle Charlie is the stingiest (most generous) person in the world.
Reason:	A. _____
Example:	1. _____
Example:	2. _____
Reason:	B. _____
Example:	1. _____
Example:	2. _____
Reason:	C. _____
Example:	1. _____
Example:	2. _____
Concluding Sentence:	In conclusion, if you are invited out by Uncle Charlie, be sure to bring your wallet with you (leave your wallet at home).

Transition Signals with Reasons

When you give reasons, you should introduce each one with a transition signal. You can use the listing-order transition signals: *first, first of all, second, third, finally,* and so forth.

> a. <u>First of all,</u> Costa Rica has an excellent system of national parks.
> <u>Second,</u> Costa Rica has many beautiful beaches.

You can also put the transition word in the subject (without commas), like this:

> b. The <u>first</u> reason is . . .
> The <u>second</u> reason is . . .

There are two ways to complete the **b** sentences above.

With a noun phrase: The first reason is <u>the excellent system of national parks</u>.

The second reason is <u>Costa Rica's beautiful beaches</u>.

With a sentence connected by *that*: The first reason is <u>that Costa Rica has an excellent system of national parks</u>.

The second reason is <u>that Costa Rica has many beautiful beaches</u>.

Remember not to use a comma when the transition signal is included in the subject.

PRACTICE:
Transition Signals with Reasons

Work with a partner or a group.

Here are three more reasons that Costa Rica is a good place to visit. Rewrite each reason twice to add transition signals.

1. Use a listing-order transition signal as in the **a** examples above. Be sure to use a comma.

2. Include the transition signal in the subject as in the **b** examples. Don't use a comma.

Reason 3:

San José, the capital, has a pleasant climate.

a. _____

b. _____

(continued on the next page)

Reason 4:

Hotels and restaurants are inexpensive.

a. _____

b. _____

Reason 5:

The people are friendly to tourists.

a. _____

b. _____

Transition Signals with Examples

There are three transition signals used to introduce examples.

TRANSITION SIGNALS WITH EXAMPLES

For example, _____ (+ sentence) _____
For instance, _____ (+ sentence) _____
_____ **such as** _____ (+ noun) _____

<u>For example,</u> visitors can watch sea turtles come ashore to lay their eggs in the sand in Tortuguero National Park.

<u>For instance,</u> the beaches at Manuel Antonio National Park are among the most beautiful in the world.

Visitors can see rare birds <u>such as</u> toucans and quetzals, and they can observe exotic animals <u>such as</u> spider monkeys.

For example and *for instance* have exactly the same meaning and are used in exactly the same way. Put them at the beginning of the sentence and put a comma after them. Examples introduced by *for example* and *for instance* must be in complete sentences.

Wrong: The restaurant specializes in seafood, for example, fresh lobster and salmon.

Right: The restaurant specializes in seafood. For example, it serves fresh lobster and salmon.

Such as is different from *for example* and *for instance. Such as* is followed by a noun. It comes in the middle of a sentence and does not need a comma.

> Tourist attractions <u>such as</u> the Eiffel Tower and museums <u>such as</u> the Louvre make Paris a favorite tourist city.

Remember these punctuation rules:

> Use commas after *for example* and *for instance.*
> Do not use a comma with *such as.*

PRACTICE:
for example, for
instance, such as

Fill in the blanks with *for example, for instance,* or *such as.* Add commas where necessary.

Example:
Denmark has many attractions for children _____such as_____ Tivoli Gardens and Legoland.

1. In São Paulo, there is a mix of architecture. You can see traditional architecture in buildings _____ the Martinelli Building and Banco do Estado de São Paulo.

2. There are also many modern buildings in São Paulo. _____ the Banco Sumitomo and Conjunto Nacional are very modern in design.

3. Tokyo's gardens are very beautiful. _____ Hibiya Park is a popular place for tourists to visit.

4. San Francisco has several ethnic[1] neighborhoods _____ North Beach (Italian), the Mission District (Hispanic), and Chinatown (Chinese).

(continued on the next page)

---

[1]**ethnic:** of different cultures, races, and nationalities

5. When you visit the ethnic neighborhoods of Miami, you feel that you are in a foreign country. _____ in Little Havana you can easily imagine that you are in Cuba.

6. Small Caribbean islands _____ Trinidad and Tobago are popular honeymoon locations.

7. Summers are much cooler in San Francisco than in Los Angeles. _____ the average July temperature in San Francisco is about 65°F, but it is 85°F in Los Angeles.

8. Mexico has many luxury beach resorts _____ Cancún and Cozumel.

9. Mexico's Yucatan Peninsula is full of archaeological treasures. _____ the Mayan ruins near Mérida are very well known.

WRITING PRACTICE 1 *Using Examples*

Work first by yourself. Then edit your paragraph with a partner.

Write a paragraph from the outline that you developed in the activity on page 137.

1. Use the same topic sentence, and add a concluding sentence.

2. Use transition signals for your main points and for your examples. Try to use *for example, for instance,* and *such as* at least once.

3. Edit your paragraph with a partner, using the Paragraph Checklist on the next page.

4. Write a neat final draft to hand in to your teacher.

PARAGRAPH CHECKLIST

FORM

✔ ✔   Check the paragraph form. (Does the paragraph look like the model on page 4?)

ORGANIZATION

☐ ☐   Does the paragraph begin with a topic sentence and end with a concluding sentence?

☐ ☐   Does the paragraph have examples to support each main point?

☐ ☐   Are the main points and examples introduced by transition signals?

☐ ☐   Does the paragraph have unity? (no irrelevant sentences)

GRAMMAR AND MECHANICS

☐ ☐   Check the capital letters.

☐ ☐   Check the spelling.

☐ ☐   Check the commas.

☐ ☐   Is there a period at the end of all the sentences?

SENTENCE STRUCTURE

☐ ☐   Check the sentences. Do they have at least one subject and one verb, and do they express a complete thought?

☐ ☐   Does the paragraph contain both simple and compound sentences?

☐ ☐   Check for comma splices and run-ons.

PART 2 Sentence Structure

In Units 1–4, you learned about simple and compound sentences. A third kind of English sentence is a **complex sentence.** Before we study these, let's learn about clauses.

Independent and Dependent Clauses

A **clause** is a group of words that contains a subject and a verb. There are two kinds of clauses in English: **independent clauses** and **dependent clauses.**

Independent clause	It rained.
Dependent clause	. . . because it rained . . .

An **independent clause** has one SV combination and expresses a complete thought. It can be a sentence by itself. A simple sentence is an independent clause.

> Paris has excellent art museums.
>
> It was cold and windy yesterday.
>
> We finished our homework and cleaned up the kitchen.

A **dependent clause** is an independent clause with a subordinating conjunction added to the beginning of it.

> . . . because it has excellent art museums . . .
>
> . . . although it was cold and windy yesterday . . .
>
> . . . after we finished our homework and cleaned up the kitchen . . .

A dependent clause does not express a complete thought, so it is not a sentence by itself. It needs to be joined to an independent clause to make sense.

Independent Clause	Dependent Clause

Art students should visit Paris <u>because it has excellent art museums.</u>

We went on a hike <u>although it was cold and windy yesterday.</u>

We watched TV <u>after we finished our homework and cleaned up the kitchen.</u>

Subordinating Conjunctions

There are many **subordinating conjunctions.** Some introduce reasons, some introduce times, and others introduce contrasts and conditions. A few of them are listed below, and a more complete list is in Appendix B.

SUBORDINATING CONJUNCTIONS

Reason	Time		Contrast	Condition
because	before	when	although	if
	after	while		

We cancelled our picnic **because** it rained.

Wait for a green light **before** you cross the street.

I will go straight to bed **after** I finish this exercise.

Where were you **when** I called?

My neighbors were having a party **while** I was trying to sleep.

My father doesn't speak English **although** he lived in England for many years.

I will be happy **if** I win the lottery.

Here are some things to remember about subordinating conjunctions:

1. A few subordinating conjunctions are also prepositions.

> **after** my accident *(preposition)*
>
> **after** I had an accident *(subordinating conjunction)*
>
> **before** class *(preposition)*
>
> **before** class begins *(subordinating conjunction)*

2. *Because* is a subordinating conjunction. *Because of* is a two-word preposition.

> **because of** my accident *(preposition)*
>
> **because** I had an accident *(subordinating conjunction)*

3. *Although* introduces a contrast or opposite. It has about the same meaning as *but.*

> **Although** they didn't study, they passed the test. *(They didn't study, but they passed the test anyway.)*
>
> **Although** I was tired, I couldn't go to sleep. *(I was tired, but I couldn't go to sleep.)*
>
> **Although** the weather was bad, they went on a picnic. *(The weather was bad, but they went on a picnic anyway.)*

4. *If* introduces a condition.

> **If** you don't study, you will fail the test.
> **If** it rains, we will cancel our picnic.
> **If** you visit my country, you should spend several days in the capital.

PRACTICE:
*Independent and
Dependent Clauses*

Work with a partner.

1. Write **IC** (independent clause) or **DC** (dependent clause) in the space
to the left of each group of words.

2. If it is a **DC,** circle the subordinating conjunction.

Example:

_DC_   (While) the class was taking a test.

_____ **1.** I take a walk around the block.

_____ **2.** Before I go to work.

_____ **3.** This exercise wakes up my body and clears my mind.

_____ **4.** It's hard to do this in the winter.

_____ **5.** Because it is still dark when I go to work.

_____ **6.** Although I try to get up early even on weekends.

_____ **7.** I sometimes sleep late on Saturdays.

_____ **8.** When it is raining, of course.

_____ **9.** I never go out.

_____ **10.** I become moody and depressed.

_____ **11.** If I don't exercise for several days.

Complex Sentences

Now let's learn about complex sentences.

> A **complex sentence** has one independent clause and one or more
> dependent clauses.

The clauses in a complex sentence can be in any order. If the dependent clause is first, put a comma after it.

Marta always gets A's <u>because she studies hard</u>.
<u>Because Marta studies hard</u>, she always gets A's.

I will quit my job immediately <u>if I win the lottery</u>.
<u>If I win the lottery</u>, I will quit my job immediately.

We went home <u>after the dance ended</u>.
<u>After the dance ended</u>, we went home.

We can write the formulas for simple, compound, and complex sentences as follows:

Simple sentence	=	**IC**		
Compound sentence	=	**IC,**	**coord. conj.**	**IC**
Complex sentence	=	**IC**	**DC**	**(no comma)**
	OR	**DC,**	**IC**	**(comma)**

PRACTICE:
Complex Sentences

Work with a partner.

A. 1. Underline the independent clauses with a <u>solid</u> line and the dependent clauses with a <u>broken line</u>.

2. Draw a circle around the subordinating conjunction.

3. Add a comma if one is needed.

Example:
(After) I won the lottery last year, my wife and I traveled around the world.

1. We were very excited when we won the lottery.[1]

2. After we got our first payment we started planning our trip.

3. We decided to visit Italy first because our parents came from there.

4. Before we left on our trip we wrote to our cousins in Rome.

5. Although we didn't know our Italian cousins they invited us to stay with them.

(continued on the next page)

---

[1]**lottery:** a gambling game

6. We studied Italian for several months before we left on our trip.

7. Although we could understand a little Italian we couldn't speak it.

8. Of course, our Italian cousins couldn't speak English although they could understand it.

9. When we arrived in Rome they met us at the airport.

10. They waited outside while the Italian officials checked our passports and luggage.

11. Finally, after we got our suitcases we went outside and met our relatives.

12. It was very confusing because no one could understand anyone.

13. However, before we left Italy we could speak a little more Italian.

14. If we go to Italy again we won't be so nervous.

B. Combine an independent clause from column A with a dependent clause from column B to make complex sentences. Write your sentences on the lines on page 153. You can write the clauses in either order, but be sure to punctuate them correctly.

A

1. Before my two brothers and I got to the lake

2. Because we forgot our fishing licenses

3. Although my brothers love fishing

4. When I am on a boat

5. After we had been fishing for a while

6. Before we could get back to shore

7. While my brothers were catching fish after fish

8. If my brothers invite me to go fishing again

B

a. I always get seasick

b. It was almost noon

c. I wasn't catching anything except a cold

d. It started to rain hard

e. We had to drive back ten miles and buy new ones

f. I hate it

g. I will say "No, thanks!"

h. We were wet from head to foot

1. _____

   _____

2. _____

   _____

3. _____

   _____

4. _____

   _____

5. _____

   _____

6. _____

   _____

7. _____

   _____

8. _____

   _____

c. Turn back to the practice on clauses on page 150. Write complex sentences by combining independent clauses with dependent clauses as follows.

Combine 1 and 2: _____

_____

Combine 4 and 5: _____

_____

Combine 6 and 7: _____

_____

(continued on the next page)

Combine 8 and 9: _____

_____

Combine 10 and 11: _____

_____

Summary: Kinds of Sentences

Let's summarize what you have learned about the three kinds of sentences.

- A **simple sentence** has one independent clause.

    It was a sunny day.

- A **compound sentence** has two or more independent clauses joined by a comma and a coordinating conjunction.

    It was a sunny day, so we went to the beach.

- A **complex sentence** has one independent and one or more dependent clauses. A comma is needed if the dependent clause comes first.

    We went to the beach because it was a sunny day.
    Because it was a sunny day, we went to the beach.

PRACTICE:

Simple, Compound, and Complex Sentences

Work by yourself or with a partner.

1. Underline all independent clauses with a <u>solid line</u> and all dependent clauses with a <u>broken line</u>.

2. In the space at the left, write the words **simple, compound,** or **complex** to identify each sentence type.

UNUSUAL VACATIONS

complex   **1.** Some people like to relax and do nothing when they take a vacation.

_____   **2.** Other people like to travel, and still others like to have an adventure.

_____ **3.** Unusual vacations are becoming popular.

_____ **4.** For example, people go hiking in Nepal or river rafting in Ecuador.

_____ **5.** Some people spend their vacations learning, and some spend their vacations helping others.

_____ **6.** A friend of mine studied Japanese during his vacation because his company is going to send him to Japan to work.

_____ **7.** A friend of mine likes to help people, so he spent his summer helping to build a school in Bangladesh.

_____ **8.** After he returned home, he wanted to go back to build a medical clinic.

_____ **9.** The travel business is changing because people are taking different vacations.

_____ **10.** After people have been in the jungles of Guatemala, they may find the beaches of Florida a little boring.

Fragments

Another kind of sentence error is called a fragment. The word **fragment** means a part of something. A sentence fragment is a part of a sentence or a piece of a sentence; it is not a whole sentence.

These are fragments:

Fragment: Because he wants to go to college.

Fragment: When the storm ended.

Fragment: Although he studies very hard.

Why are they fragments? They are fragments because they are dependent clauses. A dependent clause cannot be a sentence by itself. It must be joined to an independent clause.

Corrected: Because he wants to go to college, he studies hard.

Corrected: We went outside when the storm ended.

Corrected: Although he studies very hard, he doesn't get good grades.

Corrected: We went outside when the storm ended.

Corrected: Although he studies very hard, he doesn't get good grades.

It is especially easy to write fragments when you begin a sentence with the word *because*. For example, the paragraph above might have been written incorrectly like this (the fragment is underlined):

Why are they fragments? <u>Because they are dependent clauses.</u>
A dependent clause cannot be a sentence by itself. It must be joined to an independent clause.

It seems repititious to repeat the words *They are fragments,* but this independent clause is necessary to make the sentence complete.

PRACTICE:
Fragments

Work by yourself or with a partner.

1. Read each sentence. Decide if it is a fragment or a sentence. Write F for fragment and S for sentence.

2. Then correct each fragment by adding an independent clause. Write your new sentences on the lines below.

_____ **1.** Because several students were not prepared for the quiz.

_____ **2.** Every night, after I finish dinner.

_____ **3.** Because my children were sick, I was up all night.

_____ **4.** Because I was up all night with my sick children.

_____ **5.** Because my children were sick and I was up all night.

_____ **6.** When my children get sick.

_____ **7.** My children seem to get sick only when I have a test.

_____

_____

_____

_____

WRITING PRACTICE 2 *Sentence Combining*

Work with a partner or by yourself.

1. Combine the sentences in each group to make one sentence. Some of your sentences will be simple, some will be compound, and some will be complex. Punctuate each sentence carefully.

2. Write the sentences together as a paragraph.

CAMPING

1. a. I love to go camping.
   b. I love this in the summer.
   c. I hate to sleep on the ground.
   d. The ground is hard.
   (Use although *in front of 1a.)*

2. a. I get up in the morning.
   b. I can hardly move.
   (Use when *in front of 2a.)*

3. a. My back hurts.
   b. My muscles ache.

4. a. We go camping.
   b. We always forget something.
   (Use when *in front of 4a.)*

5. a. We forgot to bring our tent.
   b. This happened last year.
   c. We had to sleep in the open.[1]
   (Use so *in front of 5c.)*

6. a. I didn't sleep at all.
   b. I am afraid of snakes.
   c. I am afraid of bears.
   (Use because *in front of 6b.)*

7. a. I see a snake.
   b. I scream.
   c. I run.
   (Use if *in front of 7a.)*

(continued on the next page)

---

[1]**in the open:** outside

    c. I run.
       (Use if *in front of 7a.)*

8. a. I see a bear.
    b. I am frozen with fear.
       (Use if *in front of 8a.)*

9. a. I don't know why I continue to go camping every year.
    b. I really don't enjoy it.
       (Use because *in front of 9b.)*

PART 3

Grammar and Mechanics

Commas: Four More Rules

So far, you have learned these four comma rules:

Use a comma:	
1. After introductory transition signals (any transition word or phrase in front of the subject of the first independent clause)	First, carry out the empty bottles and cans. From my window, I have a beautiful view. After lunch, my grandfather takes a nap. For example, some teachers give pop quizzes.
2. To separate the items in a series	In our class there are students from Mexico, Japan, Vietnam, Iran, China, and Guatemala.
3. After the first part of a compound sentence	Cook the rice over low heat for twenty minutes, but don't let it burn. Many students work, so they don't have time to do homework.
4. After a dependent clause in a complex sentence	Because Mexico City is surrounded by mountains, it has a lot of smog.

Here are four more comma rules:

RULES	**EXAMPLES**
Use a comma:	
5. To separate thousands, millions, billions, etc.	The world's population will be more than 6,000,000,000 in the year 2000.
BUT NOT in a number that expresses a year, and NOT to separate dollars from cents or whole numbers from decimals (use a period, not a comma)	1996 $59.95 $6\frac{7}{8} = 6.875$
6. To separate the parts of dates and after years	December 31, 1999, will be the last day of this millennium.
7. To separate the parts of an address EXCEPT between the state and the zip code	The address of the White House is 1600 Pennsylvania Avenue, Washington, DC 20500.
8. After the greeting and closing in a personal letter, and after the closing in a business letter	Dear Michiko, Dear Mom, Love, Very truly yours,

PRACTICE:
Commas

A. Add commas to the sentences. (Not all sentences need them.)

Rules 1–4:

1. Some students work full time and go to school part time.

2. For example one of my classmates takes six units and works forty hours a week.

3. Because he is also married and has two children he is a very busy person.

4. He works at night attends class in the morning and sleeps when he can.

5. When he fell asleep in class yesterday we decided not to wake him up.

6. Scientists believe that animals can think feel and communicate just as humans can.

7. My dog certainly acts like a human at times.

8. For instance when he does something bad he looks guilty.

9. He hangs his head drops his tail looks up at me with sad eyes and whines.[1]

10. Later we discover the reason for his guilty looks but it's hard to punish him.

Rules 1–7:

11. The population of Mexico City will be more than 31000000 by the year 2000.

12. Astronomers believe that the Earth is 15000000000 years old.

13. My mother lives in Miami Florida in the winter and in Denver Colorado in the summer.

14. When it becomes too hot in Florida she moves to Colorado.

15. She moves back to Florida when it gets too cold in Colorado.

16. Her address in Florida is P.O. Box 695 Miami Florida 33167 and her address in Colorado is 3562 State Street Apt. 3-C Denver Colorado 80210.

---

[1]**whines:** cries

17. On Sunday June 15 1998 I graduated from college.

18. Then on Monday June 16 1998 I started looking for a job.

B. Work by yourself and then with a partner. Write one sentence of your own for Rules 1–7, but leave out the commas. Then give your seven sentences to your partner and ask him or her to put in the commas.

1. _____

_____

2. _____

_____

3. _____

_____

4. _____

_____

5. _____

_____

6. _____

_____

7. _____

_____

Capitalization: Two More Rules

Here are two more capitalization rules:

RULES	EXAMPLES

Capitalize:

11. Abbreviations

IBM NYC UCLA
VW TV CBS
USA UAE UK

> NOTE 1: USA is an abbreviation for United States of America. Do not capitalize all of the letters in a country's name.

United **S**tates of **A**merica
Saudi **A**rabia
Japan

> NOTE 2: Capitalize only the first letter of the abbreviation of a person's title.

Dr.   **M**r. and **M**rs.   **P**rof.

12. All the words in a greeting and the first word in the closing of a letter

Dear **S**ir:
To **W**hom **I**t **M**ay **C**oncern:
Love,
Very truly yours,

PRACTICE:
Capitalization Review

Work with a partner or by yourself. Review the rules for using capital letters on pages 13 and 55–56. Then change the small letters to capital letters wherever necessary in the letter from Nicole to her sister Miki.

september 3, 19__

dear miki,

   well, here i am in new york city. i still can't believe that i'm actually here! i arrived on saturday after a long flight from paris on air france. the food was excellent, and so was the movie. we saw gone with the wind. i stayed saturday and sunday nights at the fairmount hotel near rockefeller center. then on monday i moved into my dormitory at nyu.[1]

---

[1]**nyu:** New York University

i spent my entire first weekend here sightseeing. i saw many famous places: rockefeller center, the world trade center, the guggenheim museum, the ny stock exchange, and the statue of liberty. i window-shopped at gucci and saks on fifth avenue. i also visited another famous art museum and the nbc television studios.

today is a holiday in the united states. it is labor day, so all of the government offices, schools, and banks are closed. americans celebrate the end of summer by having a three-day weekend. many new yorkers spend the day in central park or go to the beach on long island.

i learned some interesting things about new york. its nickname is "the big apple," but no one knows why it's called an apple and not a banana or an orange. another interesting fact is that the first europeans who came here bought manhattan island[2] from the indians for only $24.00. of course, it's now worth trillions of dollars.

well, that's all for now. classes begin next week. i'm having a good time, but i miss you all, and i really miss french food. write soon.

with love,
nicole

Personal Letter Form

A personal letter is a letter to a friend or to a family member. To make sure the form of your personal letter is correct, do the following:

1. Write the date in the upper right-hand corner.

2. Capitalize all the words in a greeting and the first word in the closing.

---

[2]**manhattan island:** the island on which New York City is located

3. Put a comma after the greeting and after the closing.

4. Start the closing and your signature in about the middle of the page.

5. There are several possible closings for personal letters. They are listed below, in order from very friendly to formal:

> *Love,* (or) *With love,*
> *With warm regards,*
> *With regards* , (or) *With best regards,*
> *Sincerely,*

WRITING PRACTICE 3 *A Personal Letter*

Work on your own. Choose topic A or B.

Write a letter to a friend in another country. Use the letter on pages 162–163 as a model.

- Use specific names of specific places so that you practice the rules for capitalizion.
- Use simple, compound, and complex sentences in your letter.
- After you have finished writing your letter, edit it with a classmate.

Topic A

Tell your friend about your life here: for example, where you live, where you go to school, where you work, where you go on weekends. Tell this friend about some of the interesting places to visit in your area.

Topic B

Your friend is coming for a visit. You will take a week's vacation in order to show this friend the area. Plan a week's activities and write to your friend about the plan. What will you do every day? Where will you go? What interesting places will you take your friend to see?

LETTER CHECKLIST

FORM

✔ ✔ Check the letter form. (Does the paragraph look like the model on pages 162–163?)

☐ ☐ Is the date in the upper right-hand corner?

☐ ☐ Check the greeting and closing for capital letters.

☐ ☐ Check the greeting and closing for commas.

☐ ☐ Are the closing and signature in the right place?

GRAMMAR AND MECHANICS

☐ ☐ Check for capital letters.

☐ ☐ Check the spelling.

☐ ☐ Check the commas.

☐ ☐ Is there a period at the end of all the sentences?

SENTENCE STRUCTURE

☐ ☐ Check the sentences. Do they have at least one subject and one verb, and do they express a complete thought?

☐ ☐ Does the paragraph contain simple, compound, and complex sentences?

☐ ☐ Check for comma splices, run-ons, and fragments.

PART **4** The Writing Process

In this section, you will write a paragraph about a place in your home country. First, answer these questions to see if you have learned the main points of Unit 5.

REVIEW QUESTIONS

1. Organization
- What three transition signals introduce examples?
- How are they punctuated?

2. Sentence Structure
- What is an independent clause? A dependent clause?
- What are subordinating conjunctions?
- What is a complex sentence?
- How do you punctuate a complex sentence?
- What is a sentence fragment, and how can you correct one?

3. Grammar and Mechanics
- What four new comma rules did you learn?
- What two new capitalization rules did you learn?
- What is the form for a personal letter?

WRITING PRACTICE **4** *Using Reasons and Examples*

Work by yourself.

Pretend that you work for a travel agency. Write a paragraph advertising your hometown, your country's capital city, or your entire country as a great place for a vacation. Give two or three reasons why a tourist would enjoy visiting there. Give specific examples for your reasons. Use the paragraph on page 138 as a model.

First, brainstorm together with a classmate or a group of classmates from your country to get ideas. Then work alone to develop an outline and to write the first draft. Finally, edit your paragraph with a classmate.

STEP 1: *Prewrite to Get Ideas*	Get ideas by freewriting, brainstorming, or clustering. Try to find one to four reasons and at least one specific example for each reason.
STEP 2: *Outline to Organize the Ideas*	Then make an outline for your paragraph. Your outline should include a topic sentence, two to four main points, at least one specific example for each point, and a concluding sentence. It should be similar to the outline on page 139.
STEP 3: *Write the First Draft*	Write the first draft. Be sure to use transition signals.
STEP 4: *Edit the First Draft*	Edit your paragraph with a partner as you have done in previous units. Use the Paragraph Checklist below.
STEP 5: *Write the Final Draft*	Write a neat final draft to hand in to your teacher.

PARAGRAPH CHECKLIST

FORM

 ☑ ☑ Check the paragraph form. (Does the paragraph look like the model on page 4?)

ORGANIZATION

☐ ☐ Does the paragraph begin with a topic sentence and end with a concluding sentence?

☐ ☐ Does the paragraph contain at least two main reasons and at least one specific example for each reason?

☐ ☐ Do transition signals introduce the reasons and examples?

☐ ☐ Does the paragraph have unity? (no irrelevant sentences)

(continued on the next page)

PARAGRAPH CHECKLIST

GRAMMAR AND MECHANICS

☐ ☐   Check for capital letters.

☐ ☐   Check the spelling.

☐ ☐   Check the commas.

☐ ☐   Is there a period at the end of all the sentences?

SENTENCE STRUCTURE

☐ ☐   Check the sentences. Do they have at least one subject and one verb, and do they express a complete thought?

☐ ☐   Does the paragraph contain simple, compound, and complex sentences?

☐ ☐   Check for comma splices, run-ons, and fragments.

ADDITIONAL WRITING

1. A friend has written you a letter asking your advice about which school to attend. Write a letter to your friend recommending a school. Why is it a good school? What are the reasons he or she should attend it? Some factors to consider are:

size of the classes	quality of the teaching
convenient location	friendliness of the teachers
beauty of the campus	friendliness of the students
facilities (laboratories, gymnasiums, etc.)	

   Be sure to give some specific examples to support your reasons.

2. Write a review of a good restaurant in your area that serves food from your country. Use reasons and examples for support.

   First, make an outline like the one on page 139. In your outline, list at least three reasons the restaurant is excellent. Here are some factors to consider:

quality of food	service
size of portions	decor (furniture, decorations, lighting, etc.)
price	variety of choices on the menu
cleanliness	

   Include at least one example for each reason.

3. Write about a horrible restaurant in your area. Your paragraph may be serious or humorous.

4. A friend has asked you what kind of car to buy. Make a recommendation, and give reasons for your recommendation. Support your reasons with examples.

5. Write a paragraph about what you have learned in Unit 5.

Unit 6 Expressing Your Opinion

ORGANIZATION

- *Facts and Opinions*

- *Transition Signals for Opinions*

SENTENCE STRUCTURE AND GRAMMAR

- *Adjective Clauses with* who, which, *and* that

- *Sentence Fragments (continued)*

MECHANICS

- *Punctuating Adjective Clauses*

- *Business Letter Form*

THE WRITING PROCESS

Prewriting

In everyday life, people have opinions and talk about them. Should abortion be legal or illegal? Are you for or against the death penalty? At what age should a person be allowed to buy and drink alcohol or cigarettes? Should smoking be allowed in public places? These are issues which people talk about and say their opinions.

People also write their opinions. If you look at the "Letters to the Editor" section of any newspaper or magazine, you will find letters from people discussing their points of view. In class, you will often have to defend your opinions. In this unit, you will learn how to do this.

ACTIVITY

Work with a partner or small group.

1. Read the newspaper story on page 173 several times. Make sure you understand all the words and sentences.

2. Then, look at the grid on page 174 and discuss this question with your partner or group: Should the judge allow Gregory to divorce his parents?
   - Make a list of *yes* reasons if you agree.
   - Make a list of *no* reasons if you don't agree.
   - Support each reason. As support, use information from the newspaper story or use information from your own knowledge and experience.

   Here are some points to discuss:
   - What kind of parent is Rachel Kingsley?
   - Does a biological parent have more rights to his or her child than an adoptive parent?

BOY DIVORCES PARENTS

Twelve-year-old Gregory Kingsley is in court asking a judge to give him a divorce from his natural mother and father. He wants his foster parents,[1] George and Lizabeth Russ, to adopt[2] him.

Gregory's lawyers say that Gregory's natural mother, Rachel Kingsley, has not taken good care of him. They say that she abandoned[3] him because she sent him to live with relatives and foster parents.

Gregory has lived for many years as a foster child. Gregory tells the judge that his mother is cold and doesn't seem to care about him. He says that for many years, his mother sent him no cards, no letters, no Christmas gifts, and no birthday presents.

"I thought she forgot about me," he says.

Other people describe Rachel Kingsley as a person who abuses[4] drugs and alcohol. They say that she spent more time partying with male visitors than she spent with Gregory and his two younger

Gregory Kingsley

brothers. They also say that she sometimes hit the children.

Gregory says that she kept marijuana in a brown box in the living room. He also says, "She stayed out all night and brought her friends home and drank. We never had enough money, and sometimes we didn't have food."

Mrs. Kingsley says she tries to be a good mother. She says she had to send Gregory away for a while because she didn't have enough money to take care of him. At the time, she didn't have a job. Now she has two jobs, and she is living near

her parents, who can help her take care of the children.

She thought it would be better for Gregory to live with a foster family while she was having financial problems, but she never wanted him to be away from her and his brothers permanently. She says, "I thought that if I worked hard, he would be returned to me."

Her lawyer says that Rachel Kingsley's problems were temporary and that she is trying to become a responsible parent. He also says that the rights of a natural family to remain together are stronger than the rights of a foster family.

Her father believes that she has learned from her mistakes and should be given a second chance.

Rachel Kingsley

---

[1]**foster parents:** parents who are paid by the government to take care of children when their own parents cannot

[2]**adopt:** become the legal parents of

[3]**abandoned:** left behind

[4]**abuses:** uses in a wrong or bad way

Should the judge allow Gregory to divorce his parents?

YES, the judge should allow Gregory to divorce his mother.	NO, the judge should not allow Gregory to divorce his mother.
A. Reason: _____ _____ Support: _____ _____ _____ _____	A. Reason: _____ _____ Support: _____ _____ _____ _____
B. Reason: _____ _____ Support: _____ _____ _____ _____	B. Reason: _____ _____ Support: _____ _____ _____ _____
C. Reason: _____ _____ Support: _____ _____ _____ _____	C. Reason: _____ _____ Support: _____ _____ _____ _____

PART *1* Organization

Facts and Opinions

In this unit, you will express an opinion and then support that opinion with facts. Opinions are statements of someone's belief. When you say, "I believe . . . " or "I think that . . . ," you are expressing your opinion. Opinions are different from facts. People can disagree with opinions. Facts are true statements that no one can disagree with.

Read these sentences. Which ones are facts, and which ones are opinions?

The sun rises in the east.	The sunrise was beautiful this morning.
The temperature of the lake is 55°F.	The lake is too cold for swimming.
Women have fewer fatal automobile accidents than men.	Women are better drivers than men.
Women could not vote in the United States until 1920.	Everyone should vote.
Mrs. Kingsley said, "I am a good mother."	Mrs. Kingsley is a good mother.

The sentences on the left side are facts. They are true. Even the last sentence, "Mrs. Kingsley said, 'I am a good mother,'" is a fact. It is a fact that she said this. What she said—"I am a good mother"—is an opinion, but the fact is that Mrs. Kingsley said something. No one can disagree with the fact that she said something.

The sentences in the right column are opinions. People can disagree with them. They may or may not be true.

When you write an opinion paragraph, your topic sentence is an opinion. You can support your topic sentence with both opinions and facts. It is better to use facts, but it is possible to use opinions. Your paragraph will be stronger if you use more facts, however.

MODEL PARAGRAPH

Read the model on the next page and study its organization.

Capital Punishment[1]

In my opinion, capital punishment is wrong. First of all, I believe that it is wrong to kill. Only God has the right to take away life. Human beings should not kill human beings. Even if a criminal has committed horrible crimes, the government does not have the right to execute[2] him or her. Second, the threat of going to the electric chair or to the gas chamber does not stop criminals. When people commit a violent crime such as murder, they are not thinking about their punishment. In fact, many murders happen when people are angry. They are not thinking about the consequences of their actions. According to a report in the New York Times, the State of Louisiana executed eight men in nine weeks in the fall of 1987. During that same time period, the murder rate in New Orleans rose 16.4 percent. This shows that the threat of capital punishment does not stop crime. The third and most important reason for abolishing[3] the death penalty is that the government sometimes makes mistakes and executes innocent people. In fact, this has happened. According to an article in Time magazine, there were twenty-three executions of innocent people in the United States between 1900 and 1991. In my view, this makes the government itself guilty of murder. For these three reasons, I believe that the United States should get rid of capital punishment, which is really just "legal murder."

[1]**capital punishment:** the death penalty
[2]**execute:** kill legally
[3]**abolishing:** getting rid of; canceling

QUESTIONS ABOUT THE MODEL

Discuss these questions with a partner or with a group.

1. What does the writer say about capital punishment? Where does he say this? Is this a fact or an opinion?
2. How many main reasons does he give? What are the reasons? Are all the reasons facts, or is one or more of them an opinion?
3. Are all the details facts, or is one or more of them an opinion?

PRACTICE:

Outlining an Opinion Paragraph

Complete the outline for the model paragraph.

Capital Punishment

Topic Sentence: _____

_____

A. _____

_____

1. _____

_____

2. _____

_____

B. _____

_____

1. Criminals don't think about punishment while committing a crime.

2. _____

_____

C. _____

_____

1. _____

_____

Concluding Sentence: _____

_____

Transition Signals for Opinions

When you state an opinion, you should indicate that it is an opinion by using a transition expression.

> **In my opinion,** . . . . (sentence) . . . .
> **In my view,** . . . . (sentence) . . . .
>
> **I believe (that)** . . . . (sentence) . . . .
> **I think (that)** . . . . (sentence) . . . .

> In my opinion, everyone should be allowed to own a gun.
> In my view, no one should be allowed to own a gun.
> I believe that an Infiniti is better than a Lexus.
> I think a Lexus is better than an Infiniti.

Notice that the first two transitions signals are followed by commas. The second two do not have commas, and you may omit the connecting word *that*.

To give information from an outside source (a book, a newspaper, another person), use *according to* with a comma.

> **According to X,** . . . . (sentence) . . . .

> According to Gregory, his mother never wrote to him or sent him birthday cards.
> According to *Time* magazine, violence is increasing in the United States.
> According to the police, the murder happened at 11:00 P.M.

PRACTICE:
Transition Signals for Opinions

Work by yourself or with a partner.

1. Draw a circle around the transition signals for opinions in the model paragraph on page 176.

2. Draw a box around the transition signals for giving information from other sources.

PRACTICE:
Expressing Opinions

Work with a partner.

1. Write an opinion on four different topics. Use a transition signal in every sentence.

2. Then think of at least two supports for your opinion.

3. Finally, show whether each support is a fact or an opinion.

Example:

Topic: The minimum age for drinking alcohol in the United States.

Opinion: _In my opinion, there should be no minimum age for drinking alcohol._

Support: _In other countries, there is no minimum age._ (_Fact_)

Support: _Parents, not the government, should decide if their children are mature enough to drink._ (_Opinion_)

1. Topic: Smoking in public

Opinion: _____

Support: _____

_____ (_____)

Support: _____

_____ (_____)

2. Topic: Abortion

Opinion: _____

Support: _____

_____ (_____)

Support: _____

_____ (_____)

3. Topic: _____ **(Your choice)**

Opinion: _____

Support: _____

_____ (_____)

Support: _____

_____ (_____)

(continued on the next page)

4. Topic: _____ **(Your choice)**

Opinion: _____

Support: _____

_____ (_____)

Support: _____

_____ (_____)

WRITING PRACTICE 1 *Expressing an Opinion*

Work first by yourself, and then edit your paragraph with a partner. Choose one of the topics from the practice on pages 179–180 and write a paragraph about it. Use the paragraph on page 176 as a model.

STEP 1:
Prewrite to Get Ideas

Use the ideas you have already written down on pages 179–180, but add to them. Brainstorm for more reasons and details. Use the freewriting, listing, or clustering techniques to brainstorm.

STEP 2:
Outline to Organize the Ideas

Make an outline like the one on page 177. Your outline should include an opinion sentence, two to four main ideas, at least one specific example for each point, and a concluding sentence.

STEP 3:
Write the First Draft

Write the paragraph.

STEP 4:
Edit the First Draft

Edit the first draft with your partner. Use the Paragraph Checklist on the following page.

STEP 5:
Write the Final Draft

Write a neat final draft to hand in to your teacher.

PARAGRAPH CHECKLIST

FORM

☑ ☑   Check the paragraph form. (Does the paragraph look like the model on page 4?)

ORGANIZATION

☐ ☐   Does the paragraph begin with a clear opinion statement?

☐ ☐   Does the paragraph end with a concluding sentence?

☐ ☐   Is the opinion supported with at least some facts? (Remember that facts are stronger than opinions.)

☐ ☐   Are there transition signals at appropriate places?

☐ ☐   Does the paragraph have unity? (no irrelevant sentences)

GRAMMAR AND MECHANICS

☐ ☐   Check the capital letters.

☐ ☐   Check the spelling.

☐ ☐   Check the commas.

☐ ☐   Is there a period at the end of all the sentences?

SENTENCE STRUCTURE

☐ ☐   Check the sentences. Do they have at least one subject and one verb, and do they express a complete thought?

☐ ☐   Does the paragraph contain simple, compound, and complex sentences?

☐ ☐   Check for comma splices, run-ons, and fragments.

PART 2 Sentence Structure and Grammar

Adjective Clauses with who, which, *and* that

In Unit 5, you studied dependent clauses beginning with words such as *because, when, after,* and *before.* These clauses are adverb clauses because they act like adverbs. That is, they modify a verb.

There is another kind of dependent clause that begins with words such as *who, which,* and *that.* These are **adjective clauses** because they act like adjectives. That is, they modify nouns.

In the following sentences, the adjective clause is underlined with a broken line. There is a circle around *who, which,* or *that* and an arrow points to the noun that the adjective clause describes. Notice that the adjective clause comes directly after the noun it describes.

Rachel Kingsley is a person (who) abuses drugs and alcohol.

Rachel Kingsley is a person (that) abuses drugs and alcohol.

The foster parents (who) take care of Gregory want to adopt him.

The foster parents (that) take care of Gregory want to adopt him.

A box (which) was in the living room contained marijuana.

A box (that) was in the living room contained marijuana.

Here are some things to know about adjective clauses:

> **1.** Adjective clauses begin with the words *who, which,* and *that* (and others).
>
>> **who** is used for people
>> **which** is used for things
>> **that** is used for both people and things
>
> **2.** The adjective clause comes right after the noun it describes. This means that the adjective clause can come in the middle of an independent clause.
>
> **3.** Commas are sometimes used with adjective clauses, and sometimes not. (You will learn about this rule later.)

PRACTICE:
Adjective Clauses
with who, which,
and that

Work with a partner.

A. Underline the adjective clause with a broken line.

   1. Circle *who, which,* or *that.*

   2. Draw an arrow to the noun that the adjective clause describes.

   Example:

   Gregory Kingsley, who is twelve years old, wants to divorce his mother.

   1. His mother, who neglected him and his brothers, wants to keep him.

   2. He wants to be adopted by the Russes, who are his foster parents.

   3. Foster parents are people that take care of abused or neglected children.

   4. A box that contained marijuana was in the living room.

   5. The children's mother smoked marijuana, which is an illegal drug.

   6. The boys' father, who did not live with their mother, did not want the children either.

   7. This case, which was the first child-parent divorce in the United States, received a lot of attention.

   8. In my opinion, parents who don't take care of their children are criminals.

   9. The lawyer that represented Mrs. Kingsley was a woman.

  10. The judge listened carefully to both lawyers, who spoke clearly and forcefully.

B. Write *who* or *which* in the space in each sentence. (Do not use *that* in this exercise.)

ARRANGED MARRIAGES

   1. In arranged marriages, _____ are quite common in many countries, your husband or wife is chosen by someone else.

   2. Sometimes the parents, _____ know their child better than anyone, choose a marriage partner.

(continued on the next page)

3. Sometimes they hire a matchmaker, _____ is paid to find a suitable person.

4. The two young people must be very nervous at their first meeting, _____ sometimes takes place in the bride's home.

5. In some cultures, a young man or woman _____ doesn't like the parents' choice may reject him or her.

6. In other cultures, a young man or woman _____ rejects the parents' choice brings dishonor to both families.

7. Marrying "for love," _____ is the custom in some cultures, does not guarantee happiness.

8. The divorce rate is higher among people _____ marry for love.

9. People _____ listened only to their hearts sometimes wish that they had listened to their heads.

*Punctuating
Adjective
Clauses*

Sometimes you use commas with adjective clauses and sometimes you don't. Here are the rules:

> **1.** Use commas before and after an adjective clause if the noun it describes is a specific person or thing. A noun is specific if it has a name.
>
> Rachel Kingsley, who uses drugs, is not a good parent.
> Young children shouldn't see <u>Jurassic Park</u>, which has a lot of violence.
>
> **2.** Don't use commas if the noun it describes is general. A noun is general if there is no name.
>
> A person who uses drugs is not a good parent.
> Young children shouldn't see a movie which has a lot of violence.
>
> **3.** If the noun is general, you may substitute *that* for *who* and *which*. Don't use commas if the adjective clause begins with *that*.
>
> A person that uses drugs is not a good parent.
> Young children shouldn't see a movie that has a lot of violence.

PRACTICE:
Punctuating Adjective Clauses

Work with a partner.

1. Underline the adjective clause in each sentence.

2. Draw an arrow to the noun it modifies.

3. Add commas if necessary.

    1. A country that has a king or queen is called a monarchy.

    2. England which has a queen is a monarchy.

    3. A pediatrician is a doctor who takes care of children.

    4. Dr. Jones who is our neighbor is a pediatrician.

    5. Saudi Arabia and Singapore which punish criminals in public have very little crime.

    6. Countries that punish criminals in public have very little crime.

    7. Coca-Cola is a carbonated[1] drink which is sold all over the world.

    8. Coca-Cola which is sold all over the world is a carbonated drink.

    9. Millions of people drink Coca-Cola which is sold all over the world.

  10. Students that have studied regularly will do well on the final exam.

  11. Gabriela and Trinh who have studied regularly will do well on the final exam.

  12. The car that I bought yesterday broke down today.

  13. My new Supernova Sportmobile which I bought yesterday broke down today.

  14. My birthday is next Monday which is a holiday.

  15. A holiday that children especially love is Halloween.

Writing Adjective Clauses

Here's how to write sentences with adjective clauses. Remember that an adjective clause is a dependent clause. Therefore, you combine it with an independent clause to make a complete sentence.

---

[1]**carbonated:** containing CO_2

PRACTICE:
Sentences with Adjective Clauses

Work with a partner. Choose an adjective clause from the list on the right and combine it with an independent clause from the left. Several different combinations are possible. Be sure to put the adjective clause directly after the noun it describes, and add commas if necessary. Write your new sentences on the lines below.

INDEPENDENT CLAUSES

1. They gave their boss a Rolex watch.

2. The purse is hers.

3. Sandy moved to New York last month.

4. She is living in an apartment.

5. On our honeymoon we stayed at the Bellagio.

6. My Uncle John has everything.

7. A person has everything.

ADJECTIVE CLAUSES

a. who owns a house on every continent, his own private jet, and two yachts

b. which is on the thirteenth floor

c. who was celebrating his 50th birthday

d. who has love

e. who is my best friend

f. which is lying under the chair

g. which is the newest hotel in Las Vegas

1. _____

_____

2. _____

_____

3. _____

_____

4. _____

_____

5. _____

_____

6. _____

_____

7. _____

_____

PRACTICE:
Sentences with
Adjective Clauses

In this exercise, combine two simple sentences to make a complex sentence containing an adjective clause.

Work with a partner.

1. Read the two sentences in each pair. Which noun in the first sentence is the second sentence talking about? Is it a person or a thing? Find it and underline it.

2. Change the second sentence into an adjective clause by crossing out the subject and substituting _who, which,_ or _that._

3. Move the new adjective clause to its correct position (right after the underlined noun) in the first sentence.

4. Add commas if necessary.

Examples:

that (which)
This is a story. ~~It~~ appeared in the newspaper recently.

This is a story that appeared in the newspaper recently.

OR   This is a story which appeared in the newspaper recently.

who
Michael Fay was punished by caning.[1] ~~He~~ was an American high school student in Singapore.

Michael Fay, who was an American high school student in Singapore, was

punished by caning.

1. Michael Fay attended an international high school. He lived in Singapore with his mother.

_____

_____

(continued on the next page)

---
[1]**caning:** beating with a thick bamboo stick

2. Singapore has strict laws. Singapore has very little crime.

_____

_____

3. Michael Fay spray-painted some cars. The cars were parked on the street.

_____

_____

4. He went in front of a judge. The judge sentenced him to six strokes with a cane.

_____

_____

5. Some people don't agree with punishments. Some punishments cause pain.

_____

_____

6. Other people said Michael should be punished by Singapore's laws. Michael broke Singapore's laws.

_____

_____

PRACTICE:
Writing Sentences with Adjective Clauses

Work with a partner or with a group.

1. Read the story on the next page. This is a true story. It happened in 1992, in Louisiana, which is a state in the southern part of the United States. Make sure that you understand all the words. Discuss it with your group.

A TRAGIC MISTAKE—OR MURDER?

Japanese exchange student approaches the wrong house—shot to death.

The Halloween decorations—a paper skeleton and a plastic ghost—are still outside of Rodney Peairs's neat brick house in Central, Louisiana. A red bloodstain is still on the floor of the carport. The decorations are the reason a sixteen-year-old Japanese exchange student, Yoshiro Hattori, approached the house. The bloodstain is the result.

Hattori was an exchange student. He had been in the United States for three months. He lived with an American family and attended high school. His classmates described him as bright, friendly, and full of energy.

Wrong House

On the Saturday night before Halloween, young Hattori dressed himself in a tuxedo with a white jacket. With his host family's son, he went looking for a Halloween party that was being given by another Japanese student. But the two young men had the wrong address. They got lost.

When they saw Halloween decorations at the Peairs's house, they stopped and knocked. Mrs. Peairs came to the door. She was afraid. She quickly shut the door and told her husband to get his gun. The boys walked to the carport door. Peairs appeared with a gun and told them to "freeze."

But Hattori didn't understand the word *freeze* because his English was poor. *Freeze* means *stop moving*. He continued moving toward Peairs. Peairs shot him. A neighbor ran to help, but it was too late.

The shooting shocked Japan. The shooting has created a furor[1] there. Many Japanese already think that America is a land of guns and violence, and this incident proved it to them.

In Central, the people are sad and feel sorry, but they are not shocked. Central is a small town in Louisiana. Most of the people who live there are working class and white. Most people in Central have guns for hunting. In fact, guns are as common as garden hoses.

Shoot-the-Burglar Law

"White people are quick on the trigger here," said G. Washington Eames, head of the NAACP.[2] Louisiana has a "shoot-the-burglar" law. This law says that killing may be justified if a person finds a stranger inside the four walls of his house. However, it is not clear if a carport, which is only a roof over a driveway, is "four walls."

Peairs is thirty years old. He is a butcher at a local supermarket. His neighbor says he is a friendly person and is not trigger-happy.[3] "He's one of the calmest persons I know," the neighbor said. "He's very easy-going." The police say Peairs has no criminal record.

---

[1] **furor:** storm of anger

[2] **NAACP:** National Association for the Advancement of Colored People, an organization that fights racial prejudice

[3] **trigger-happy:** (slang) likes to pull the trigger of a gun; in other words, likes to shoot guns

2. Now take information from the story on page 189 and write ten new sentences containing adjective clauses. Write five sentences with *who* or *that* and five sentences with *which* or *that*.

Example:

Yoshiro Hattori, who was a student from Japan, was killed by Rodney Peairs.

1. _____

2. _____

3. _____

4. _____

5. _____

6. _____

7. _____

8. _____

9. _____

10. _____

Sentence Fragments (continued)

In Unit 5, you learned about the sentence error called a fragment. Sometimes this error happens when people write a dependent clause (or two dependent clauses) and forget to add an independent clause.

Fragment: If you want to transfer to a four-year college.

Fragment: Because it was raining when we left.

Here is another kind of sentence fragment that people may write when they use adjective clauses.

Fragment: Ron, who sometimes teaches night classes at another school.

Fragment: The book that I loaned you last week.

These are fragments because there is no independent clause. There is only a noun and a dependent adjective clause. To correct this kind of fragment, finish the independent clause.

Corrected: Ron, who sometimes teaches night classes at another school, is a busy person.

Corrected: I need to read the book that I loaned you last week.

PRACTICE:
Fixing Fragments

A. Work with a partner or by yourself.

1. Read each sentence. Decide if it is a fragment or a sentence. Write F for fragment and S for sentence.

2. Then correct each fragment by completing the independent clause. Write the corrected sentences on the lines below.

_____ **1.** Every family that lives in an earthquake area should have an earthquake plan.

_____ **2.** For example, Californians who live in certain areas.

_____ **3.** Every family should keep emergency food and water in their house.

_____ **4.** Also, a radio and a barbecue grill that they can use for cooking.

_____ **5.** Capital punishment, which is legal killing by the government.

_____ **6.** Violence has become a way of life in the United States.

_____ **7.** Television programs that children learn from.

_____ **8.** Television programs show hundreds of violent acts every day.

_____

_____

_____

_____

_____

(continued on the next page)

B. Work with a partner or by yourself.

1. Read each sentence in the following paragraph. Underline the fragments and write FRAG above them. There are eight fragments.

2. Then correct each fragment. To correct the fragments, you can write new independent clauses, or you can add the fragment to an existing independent clause. Write the corrected sentences on the lines on the next page.

Capital Punishment

FRAG

I am in favor of capital punishment. <u>First of all, when a criminal commits mass murder.</u>[1] He or she should not be allowed to live. For example, the man who killed five and wounded twenty-nine schoolchildren in Stockton, California. Also, people who are serial killers.[2] They should not be allowed to live. Because they might kill again. An example of a serial killer is John Gacy, who murdered thirty-three young men over a period of several years. Such a monster has no right to live. Second, because the families of the victims have rights, too. How would you feel if your wife or husband or child were murdered? If something is taken from you. You have the right to take something, too. The Bible says that a victim has the right to demand "an eye for an eye, and a tooth for a tooth." Third, capital punishment definitely stops crime. In countries with hard punishments, there is less crime. For example, Saudi Arabia, which beheads[3] murderers. Saudi Arabia has a very low crime rate. In conclusion, I am for capital punishment for three reasons. Because it is necessary to remove evil people from society, because it gives justice to the murder victims' families, and because it prevents more murders from happening.

---

[1]**mass murder:** the killing of many people at the same time
[2]**serial killers:** people who kill many people, one at a time, over a long period
[3]**beheads:** cuts the head off

Corrected sentences:

First of all, when a criminal commits mass murder, he or she should not be allowed to live.

Sentence Combining

Work with a partner.

1. Combine the sentences in each group. There may be more than one possible way to combine them.

2. Punctuate each sentence carefully.

3. Write the new sentences together as a paragraph.

CULTURES IN CONFLICT

1. a. Jamila Haddad ran away from home last week.
   b. She is a high school student in Chicago.

2. a. She ran away to avoid a marriage.
   b. It was arranged by her parents.

3. a. Mr. and Mrs. Haddad are very traditional.
   b. They are from Lebanon.

4. a. Jamila is the oldest daughter in the Haddad family.
   b. The Haddad family came to the United States seven years ago.

(continued on the next page)

5. a. Her parents want her to marry a man.
   b. The man is thirty-two years old.

6. a. Jamila is a good student.
   b. Jamila is eighteen.

7. a. She gets straight As.
   b. She plays basketball.
   c. She has many friends.

8. a. She doesn't have a boyfriend.
   b. Her parents won't allow it.

9. a. She wants to go to college.
   b. Her parents don't want her to.

10. a. The husband-to-be lives in Lebanon.
    b. Lebanon is a country in the Middle East.

11. a. He owns a business.
    b. The business is very successful.

12. a. People say that he is very nice.
    b. They know him.

13. a. Jamila doesn't think she can change her parents' minds.
    b. She ran away.

14. a. Mr. and Mrs. Haddad don't understand why she ran away.
    b. They have traditional values.

15. What do you think?

16. a. Should she go to Lebanon and marry the man?
    b. Should she stay in the United States and go to college?

PART 3 Mechanics

Business Letter Form

A business letter is any letter that is not personal; that is, it is a letter you write to anyone except your family and friends. Business letters in English have a special form.

Study the model and notice the location, spacing, capitalization, and punctuation of the different parts.

225 Water Street
Boston, MA 12356
December 15, 199_

(skip 4 lines)

Mr. Daniel Perotti
Perotti Imports
666 Knoll Lane
Denver, CO 30303
    (skip 1 line)
Dear Mr. Perotti:
    (skip 1 line)
    I am writing to ....
....
....
....
....
....
....
....
....
....
....
....

(skip 1 line)
Thank you very much for your time and attention.
    (skip 1 line)
                    Very truly yours,

(skip 4 lines)

David Kennedy
David Kennedy

Here are some things to learn about business letters.

> **1.** Your address and the date are in the upper right-hand corner, just as shown. The number and street are on the first line; the city, state, and zip code are on the second line; and the date is on the third line.
>
> **2.** Skip four lines between the date and the name and address of the person you are writing to. Also skip four lines between the closing and your printed (or typed) name.
>
> **3.** Skip one line between every other part of the letter, including each paragraph.
>
> **4.** A business letter usually begins with a sentence that directly states your purpose. Typical openings are *I am writing to complain . . .* or *I am writing to request . . .*
>
> **5.** A business letter usually ends with a paragraph or sentence that thanks the person. A typical ending is *Thank you for your time and attention to this matter.*
>
> **6.** Capitalize all of the words in a greeting and the first word in the closing.
>
> **7.** Put a colon (:) after the greeting and a comma after the closing.
>
> **8.** Start the closing and your signature around halfway across the page.
>
> **9.** There are several possible closings for business letters. They are listed below, in order from neutral to very formal:
>
> > *Sincerely,* (or) *Sincerely yours,*
> > *Very truly yours,*
> > *Respectfully,* (or) *Respectfully yours,*

WRITING PRACTICE 3 *A Business Letter*

Write the letter by yourself. Then edit your letter with a partner, using the checklist on the next page.

- In your first sentence, tell why you are writing. In your second sentence, state your opinion.

- In the supporting sentences, write your reasons. Support your reasons with specific details. (You may use facts from the newspaper story, and you may use information from your own knowledge and experience.)
- Write a concluding sentence. Summarize your reasons, and repeat your request.

Choose Topic A or B.

Topic A

Pretend that you are good friends of Mr. and Mrs. Russ, the foster parents of Gregory Kingsley. Write a letter to the judge who will decide the case. Ask the judge to give Gregory a divorce from his mother and to let the Russes adopt him.

Topic B

Pretend that you are Rachel Kingsley's best friend. Write a letter to the judge who will decide the case. Ask the judge to give her son back to her.

For either letter, use this fictitious[1] name and address for the judge: The Honorable Jacob B. Fenston, Judge of the Miami Municipal Court, 6 Courthouse Square, Miami, FL 01113. Use this greeting: Dear Judge Fenston:.

BUSINESS LETTER CHECKLIST

FORM

✓ ✓ Check the letter form. (Does the letter look like the model on page 195?)

☐ ☐ Is your address and the date in the upper right-hand corner?

☐ ☐ Check the greeting and closing for capital letters.

☐ ☐ Check the punctuation of the greeting and closing.

☐ ☐ Are the closing and signature in the right place? Is the writer's name printed under the signature?

(continued on the next page)

---

[1] **fictitious:** not real

BUSINESS LETTER CHECKLIST

ORGANIZATION

☐ ☐ Does the letter begin with a clear statement of the purpose of the letter?

☐ ☐ Does the second sentence state a clear opinion?

☐ ☐ Is the opinion supported with reasons?

☐ ☐ Are the reasons supported by specific supporting details?

☐ ☐ Is there a concluding sentence?

GRAMMAR AND MECHANICS

☐ ☐ Check the capital letters.

☐ ☐ Check the spelling.

☐ ☐ Check the commas.

☐ ☐ Is there a period at the end of all the sentences?

SENTENCE STRUCTURE

☐ ☐ Check the sentences. Do they have at least one subject and one verb, and do they express a complete thought?

☐ ☐ Does the paragraph contain simple, compound, and complex sentences?

☐ ☐ Check for comma splices, run-ons, and fragments.

PART 4   The Writing Process

In this section, you will write an opinion paragraph about the story "A Tragic Mistake—or Murder?" First, answer these questions to see if you have learned the main points of Unit 6.

REVIEW QUESTIONS

1. Organization
- What is the difference between a fact and an opinion?
- Can you use both facts and opinions to support an opinion?
- Which is stronger support?

2. Sentence Structure and Grammar
- What is an adjective clause?
- What are three words that can introduce an adjective clause?
- When is each word used?
- When do you use commas with an adjective clause?
- Can you use a comma with *that*?
- What kind of fragments are a danger when you write a sentence with an adjective clause?

3. Mechanics
- What is the form of a business letter?

WRITING PRACTICE 4   *Guilty or Innocent?*

First work with a group and then by yourself. Write a paragraph expressing your opinion about the story "A Tragic Mistake—or Murder?" on page 189. Use the paragraph on page 176 as a model.

STEP 1:
Prewrite to Get Ideas

Decide if you think Rodney Peairs is guilty of murder or if you believe the shooting was a tragic accident. Find two to four reasons to support your opinion. Also, discuss what specific details you can use to support your reasons.

STEP 2:
Outline to Organize the Ideas

Then make an outline. Your outline should look like the outline on page 177.

STEP 3:
Write the First Draft

Then, write your paragraph from your outline. Try to include some sentences with adjective clauses.

STEP 4:
Edit the First Draft

Edit your paragraph with a classmate, using the Paragraph Checklist below.

STEP 5:
Write the Final Draft

Write a neat final draft to hand in to your teacher.

PARAGRAPH CHECKLIST

FORM

✔ ✔ Check the paragraph form. (Does the paragraph look like the model on page 4?)

ORGANIZATION

☐ ☐ Does the paragraph begin with a topic sentence and end with a concluding sentence?

☐ ☐ Does the paragraph have at least two reasons and one specific detail for each reason?

☐ ☐ Are there transition signals at appropriate places?

☐ ☐ Does the paragraph have unity? (no irrelevant sentences)

GRAMMAR AND MECHANICS

☐ ☐ Check the capital letters.

☐ ☐ Check the spelling.

☐ ☐ Check the commas.

☐ ☐ Is there a period at the end of all the sentences?

SENTENCE STRUCTURE

☐ ☐ Check the sentences. Do they have at least one subject and one verb, and do they express a complete thought?

☐ ☐ Does the paragraph contain simple, compound, and complex sentences?

☐ ☐ Check for comma splices, run-ons, and fragments.

ADDITIONAL WRITING

1. Write a paragraph about arranged marriages and marriages "for love." Which do you think is better, and why?

2. Write a personal letter to Jamila Haddad's parents. Tell them your opinion. Do you think she should go to Lebanon and marry the man, or do you think she should stay in the United States and go to college?

3. Write a letter to the head of your school. Tell this person about a problem in the school. Give the reasons why you think it is a problem. Support your reasons with examples. Tell what you think should be done about the problem.

4. Write a paragraph about what you have learned in Unit 6.

Appendix A: Correction Symbols

p.	punctuation error	She lives in Salem, *[p.]* and works in Boston. This dessert is made with eggs *[p.]* milk *[p.]* and sugar.
agr.	faulty agreement	My brother *[agr.]* study engineering.
art.	article error	I don't have *[art.]* a time to do *[art.]* a homework. Give the money to *[art.]* robber, quickly!
cap.	capitalization error	My brother goes to *[cap.]* harvard *[cap.]* university and studies *[cap.]* Medicine. He plans to become a *[cap.]* Doctor.
⊂	join to make a compound or complex sentence	My best friend lives in Norfolk. *[⌒]* So we don't see each other often.
pl.	plural	He likes fast music, fast *[pl.]* car, and fast women.
sp.	spelling mistake	He *[sp.]* speeks Spanish and Portuguese.
v.t.	wrong verb tense	He is *[v.t.]* eating the same thing for lunch every day.
w.f.	wrong word form	She is a very nice and *[w.f.]* kindness teacher.
w.w.	wrong word	She gave the wrong *[w.w.]* factory.
◯	word missing	He ⌃ working at (the) McDonald's now.
⊘	unnecessary word	
∿	wrong word order	You never are at home when I call.

RO   run-on   We ate dinner *RO* then we went out.

        (Correction: We ate dinner. Then we went out.

           OR   We ate dinner, and then we went out.)

CS   comma splice   We ate dinner, *CS* then we went out.

        (Correction: We ate dinner. Then we went out.

           OR   We ate dinner, and then we went out.)

FRAG   fragment   *FRAG* The movie that we saw last night.

        (Correction: The movie that we saw last night was very entertaining.)

¶   paragraph   This is the symbol for paragraph.

Ⓣ   transition   Add or change a transition signal. English has many silent letters. Ⓣ The *b* in the word *doubt* is not pronounced.

        (Correction: English has many silent letters. For example, the *b* in the word *doubt* is not pronounced.)

Appendix B: Conjunctions

COORDINATING CONJUNCTIONS

for   and   nor   but   or   yet   so

SUBORDINATING CONJUNCTIONS

Adverb Clauses:	**Adjective Clauses:**
Time	**People**
after	who
as soon as	that
before	
since	**Things**
until	which
while	that
when	
whenever	

Adverb Clauses:

Reason
    as
    because
    since

Condition
    as if
    even if
    if
    unless

Contrast
    although
    even though
    though

Purpose
    in order that
    so that

Appendix C: Transition Signals

Time Order
    First, . . .
    First of all, . . .
    Second, . . .
    Third, . . .
    Next, . . .
    After that, . . .
    Then . . .
    Finally, . . .

Listing
    First, . . .
    First of all, . . .
    Second, . . .
    Third, . . .
    Fourth, . . .
    Also, . . .
    . . . also . . .
    In addition, . . .

Space Order
    On the right, . . .
    On the left, . . .
    In the center, . . .
    In the middle, . . .
    Next to the . . . , . . .
    Beside the . . . , . . .
    Between the _____ , . . .
    Opposite the _____ , . . .
    Near the _____ , . . .
    Under the _____ , . . .
    Above the _____ , . . .
    On one side of the _____ , . . .
    On the other side of the _____ , . . .

Reasons
    The first reason is (that) . . .
    The second reason is (that) . . .
    The most important reason is
        (that) . . .

Examples
    For example, . . .
    For instance, . . .
    . . . such as . . .

Opinions
    In my opinion, . . .
    In my view, . . .
    According to _____ , . . .
    I believe (that) . . .
    I think (that) . . .

Conclusions
    In brief, . . .
    In short, . . .
    For these reasons, . . .

Appendix D: Word Division

Sometimes a word is too long to fit on a line, so you must divide the word and write part of it on one line and the rest of it on the next line below (after skipping a line, of course!). Put a hyphen (-) after the first part of the word. Where should you divide a word? Here are some basic guidelines:

1. Always divide a word between syllables. If you are not sure where the syllables are, look the word up in a dictionary. A dictionary shows syllabic divisions with a small dot:

in·ter·na·tion·al	com·mu·ni·ca·tion
sci·ence	class·mate
re·write	house (cannot be divided)

   Here are two hints:

   a. Divide after a vowel:

ho·nor (*not* hon·or)	spe·cial (*not* spec·ial)
ra·pid (*not* rap·id)	deco·rate (*not* dec·orate)

   b. Divide between a double consonant (*mm, nn, ll, pp*, etc.):

col·lege	em·bar·rass
com·mute	sit·ting

   BUT keep word roots together:

tall·est	sell·ing

2. Divide hyphenated words (*part-time, mother-in-law*, only after the hyphen:

mother-in-law	(*not* mo·ther-in-law)

3. Leave at least two letters on a line. For example, don't divide these words:

e·rase	wind·y

PRACTICE:
Dividing Words

Use a dictionary to do this exercise. Work by yourself or with a partner.

1. Show with hyphens where these words can be divided. Look them up in a dictionary if you are not sure.

2. Some words cannot be divided; put an X in the space next to them.

a. divide   *di-vide*   **j.** paragraph   _____

b. letter   _____   **k.** book   _____

c. teacher   _____   **l.** bookstore   _____

d. full-time   _____   **m.** unfortunate   _____

e. read   _____X_____   **n.** reading   _____

f. student   _____   **o.** microwave   _____

g. lazy   _____   **p.** appointment   _____

h. illegal   _____   **q.** non-credit   _____

i. office   _____   **r.** businessman   _____

Appendix E: Parts of Speech

Students and teachers use special vocabulary to talk about grammar and sentence structure. Each word in a sentence has a name that tells what kind of word it is. These names are the **parts of speech.**

PARTS OF SPEECH

Noun	Names a person, place, or thing; is used as a subject or as an object	Alice, book, friendship, fear, island, Cuba *Alice wrote a book of poems for her friend.*
Pronoun	Replaces a noun	he, I, them, it, ours, yours, us, this, that *She wrote it for him.*

PARTS OF SPEECH (continued)

Verb	Tells action, feeling, condition	write, is writing, wrote, was writing, can write, has written, is going to write
		How many paragraphs <u>have</u> we <u>written</u>? *I <u>am going to write</u> a letter tonight.*
OR	Links the subject with the rest of the sentence	is, was, has been, seem, appear, feel, look, taste, smell
		The old man <u>appeared</u> to be sleeping.
		(Note: *To be* is an infinitive. It is not like a verb that can change its form.)
Article	Makes a noun specific or general	the (specific), a, an (general)
		Please take <u>a</u> seat in <u>the</u> front row.
Adjective	Describes a noun or pronoun	red, hungry, fourth, three, Cuban, afraid
		<u>Three</u> <u>daring</u> students were smoking <u>Cuban</u> cigars in the <u>school</u> office, but they weren't <u>afraid</u> of getting caught.
Adverb	Describes a verb, adjective, or another adverb; tells how, where, or when	beautifully, easily, quickly, very, too, here, there, everywhere now, then, later, often, sometimes
		The students put out their cigars <u>very</u> <u>quickly</u> and left <u>there</u> <u>immediately</u>.
Preposition	Shows a relationship such as time, location, reason	in, on, at, around, from, by, with, of, because of, next to, according to (2 words)
		The headmaster <u>of</u> the school came <u>into</u> the room and looked <u>under</u> the table <u>for</u> the students.

PARTS OF SPEECH (continued)

Coordinating conjunction	Connects equal elements	and, but, or, so, for, nor, yet *He didn't find them, <u>so</u> he left.*
Subordinating conjunction	Is the first word in a dependent clause; it makes the clause dependent	when, because, if, although, who, which, that *He didn't find them <u>because</u> they had already left.*

Practice identifying the parts of speech in any of the sentences in this book.

Index